Open More Doors. Close More Sales.

Mastering the Essentials of Sales

WHAT YOU NEED TO KNOW TO CLOSE EVERY SALE

Gerhard Gschwandtner

Founder and Publisher of Selling Power

McGraw-Hill

New York   Chicago   San Francisco   Lisbon   London
Madrid   Mexico City   Milan   New Delhi   San Juan
Seoul   Singapore   Sydney   Toronto

The *McGraw-Hill* Companies

1 2 3 4 5 6 7 8 9 0 DOC/DOC 0 9 8 7 6

ISBN 0-07-147386-6

McGraw-Hill books are available at special quantity discounts to use
as premiums and sales promotions, or for use in corporate training
programs. For more information, please write to the Director of
Special Sales, Professional Publishing, McGraw-Hill, Two Penn Plaza,
New York, NY 10121-2298. Or contact your local bookstore.

 This book is printed on recycled, acid-free paper containing a
minimum of 50% recycled, de-inked fiber.

ACKNOWLEDGMENTS

First, I would like to thank the *Selling Power* magazine readers for their positive feedback on my monthly essays. My ego soars because of your encouragement. Thanks to the entire *Selling Power* staff, past and present, for all their hard work, creative energy, commitment to quality, and dedication to serve our customers with great enthusiasm.

ABOUT THIS BOOK

I've made it my life's mission to make a positive contribution to the sales profession. Although I've written a dozen books for salespeople and sales managers, this book is dearest to my heart. When possible, I wrote each of the 51 sales essentials on a weekend when I could research, think, and write without interruption. To me, writing is like making a sales call. My objective is to sell a new idea to the reader. My goal is to help every reader win. Before I start writing, I research the subject online for several hours so that I feel well prepared. Then I work on the opening line, which may be a simple question or a statement that contains an emotional trigger. In other words, the opening has to involve the customer from the get-go. Once I get the reader's attention, I try to hold it with a persuasive presentation that is respectful of the reader's time. Sometimes I use bullet points that reveal interesting data, surprising facts, or my personal insights. To earn the reader's trust, I back up my claims with research, relevant historical connections, or compelling quotes from reliable authorities. To reduce the chance of losing the reader to indifference or boredom, I try to keep the language simple, the sentences short, and the subject in clear focus. I love nothing more than closing each essay with a memorable sentence, a call to action, or an appeal to change. To make this book more useful, I've added success principles, reminders, and action tips. If you enjoy this book, please share it with others. If you want to share your thoughts, please email me at gerhardpsp@aol.com. I always welcome your feedback.

CONTENTS

Part 1: The Basics of Sales Success

Part 2: Developing into a Sales Leader

Part 1:
The Basics of
Sales Success

1

THE STORY OF *SELLING POWER* MAGAZINE

M y copy of the first issue of *Selling Power* is a dog-eared, faded, eight-page newspaper tabloid. I remember writing the first article 21 years ago in my garage office. My vision was to give sales managers a tool to help their salespeople become more effective. I was short on money but big on dreams. I had no idea what it meant to build a publishing company. English was my third language, and I was scared to death of failing. I had no idea just how much work, self-education, and frustration would be required to turn *Selling Power* magazine into reality. Every time a new issue was printed, I went to the pressroom and checked every single copy that came off the press.

To set the record straight about the origins of *Selling Power,* I have to confess that I did not design the first issue with the idea of starting a magazine. Before the start of *Selling Power,* I was in the sales-training business, and in an effort to spend more time at home with my wife and newborn twin daughters, I created an audiovisual course called "The Languages of Selling" that I would sell through direct mail. I hired a copywriter and put together a slick, four-color brochure, rented a mailing list, and sent the direct-mail piece to 25,000 sales managers. The response was great, but my profit margin was low. So I decided to re-place the expensive brochure with an eight-page tabloid-style newspaper. I figured that the tabloid could pull as well as the brochure, at half the price.

The key was to get the busy sales manager's attention—but how? I simply shared every selling and training secret I had collected over the many years I'd been on the road selling, managing, and training. When I looked at the final layout of the publication, I thought that people would want to buy extra copies, so we added a small ad offering reprints at 65 cents each. As it turned out, we not only sold as many programs as with the slick brochure, but also filled orders for 3,000 additional copies of *Selling Power.* That was in June 1981. When we tried two months later with another edition of *Selling Power,* we raised the price to 75 cents per copy and sold more than 4,000 copies. When a third edition produced similar results, my wife suggested the idea of creating an ad offering a one-year subscription to the publication. Although I loved the idea, I was not en-tirely convinced that it would work.

I thought about it over a weekend and came up with a

plan. I said, "I'll give it a try. If we get more than 500 subscriptions, I'll continue; if we get fewer than 500, I will refund the money with a letter explaining that the idea did not work." Only 30 days after mailing 25,000 complimentary copies of *Selling Power,* we received 1,200 paid subscriptions. By the end of 1982, we had 7,500 paid subscribers. Every month, the money from new subscribers was used to

1981

expand the publication and pay the printing and postage bills.

Once we published the first few issues, *Selling Power* took on a life of its own. As we put together issue after issue, we realized that we were serving a much larger cause. Serving an army of readers can be a humbling experience. I've always had a high respect for the wisdom, the experience, and the dedication of our readers.

From the start we thought it would be foolish to consider ourselves the ultimate experts in the field, so we began to establish connections with such leading authorities as best-selling authors, famous coaches, successful entrepreneurs, respected CEOs, noted psychologists, eminent scholars, and street-smart managers. It has been a privilege to gain access to so many extraordinary people who have generously shared their time and ideas with *Selling Power.* I sometimes wonder how different my view of the

1989

world would be if I had not met with such fascinating people as General Norman Schwarzkopf, Mary Kay Ash, Zig Ziglar, Tony Robbins, President George H. W. Bush, George Foreman, John Cleese, Michael Dell, Cal Ripken Jr., Andy Grove, Hugh Downs, Donald Trump, or Larry King. Every one of these super-achievers helped me draw the blueprint for our own success.

For the first five years, the publication did not produce a profit. I sold advertising, secured key interviews, wrote cover stories, supervised every press run, created direct mail pieces, hired and trained people, and delivered a few speeches to boost our cash. Since I lacked formal training in publishing, I made many trips to the Library of Congress and immersed myself in books and other magazines. I studied the histories of *Reader's Digest, Time, The Ladies Home Journal,* and *Forbes* magazine. Over a period of 10 years, I studied more than 2,000 books on selling and managing.

I've always had faith that if we give our readers the best information, prepared in the most useful way, people will sit up and notice us; but if we hold back or grow indifferent, then people will turn away from us. Our readers recognized that we were passionate about making *Selling Power* better with every issue. Whenever we had an extra dollar, we invested it to improve the magazine. We soon upgraded the appearance of the publication: we added color, better photography, better designs, better paper—anything to enhance the quality of our product.

In 1987 we changed from newsprint to a four-color tabloid. In 1990 we went to the standard magazine format. Every time we made improvements, our circulation went up

2002

and we attracted more advertisers. Over time, our magazine has enjoyed wider distribution. Today we're sold in bookstores and on newsstands; we're on United Airlines planes and in Red Carpet Clubs. Our magazine is read in 67 countries worldwide. *Selling Power* is read in sales offices, in trains, on planes, in limousines, in waiting rooms, and in boardrooms.

Over the years, even the magazine industry took notice. *Selling Power* has received many dozens of editorial and design awards. We're very proud of this achievement.

Selling Power continues to grow, evolve, and adapt to the changing needs of our expanding customer base. Through good times and tough times, we will continue to deliver the best sales and management ideas, intelligently and with integrity, imagination, and intensity.

The ingredient most important to the life of *Selling*

Power is its readers, who have recognized the value of our editorial product and have subscribed and recommended our magazine to others. What a thrill it is to earn your support with every article. I am passionate about helping the profession of selling, and I can assure you that the best is yet to come.

$$\boxed{2}$$

THE EVOLUTION OF THE
AMERICAN SALES PROFESSION

Before the Civil War, Yankee peddlers responded to the demand for goods across the nation. To facilitate trade, America began to build better roads, which further stimulated the economy. Many of the New England peddlers were shrewd salespeople who sold tin pots and pans to colonial housewives. Some of these peddlers became wealthy merchants; others became famous for their creative selling techniques. But the "good-old days" of the peddler vanished with the appearance of the "drummer" who often competed for sales with local merchants. Many states required these drummers to purchase a license in exchange for the privilege of selling in that state. For example, in 1880 the Texas legislature passed a law requiring "drummers, fortune tellers, cock fighters and clairvoyants" to buy a license for $20.

T. J. Carey wrote about how buyers viewed the typical drummer: "I like his breezy ways, his unaffected and easy style of approach, the bits of news he brings me of trade changes and conditions. . . . He is a newspaper—market report, funny column, society and police news. . . . He is a blessed nuisance."

By 1896, there were more than 400,000 of these salespeople known as drummers in America. The proliferation of drummers gave the hotel industry a welcome boost.

E. F. Statler collected many of his ideas for building modern hotels by listening to drummers. Statler's hotels were the first to offer a private bath and a radio in every room. Statler also offered free newspapers and a quick dry-cleaning service to traveling salespeople.

At the turn of the century, the drummer was replaced by the trained salesperson, who set new records of productivity and efficiency. The driving force behind this modern salesmanship was John Henry Patterson, the founder of NCR (National Cash Register). He taught his salespeople to dress well, speak well, organize their presentations, refrain from telling funny stories, and refrain from smoking when calling on customers.

Patterson created a series of astonishingly effective systems that make some of today's sales organizations look like a loose collection of amateurs. Patterson elevated sales training to an art and a science. He hired an elocutionist to teach his salespeople to speak in public; then he collected the best sales presentations and created the first comprehensive sales manual that covered every sales process from generating leads to tested ways for handling customer objections to proven ways for closing the sale. He invented the fair quota system based on market share and created sales incentives that involved the salesperson's spouse. In 1910, NCR's employee benefits included hot lunches, two exercise breaks each day, supervised child care, and a country club membership.

REMINDER

The progress of America's economy has always depended on salespeople who had the courage to take an idea and make something out of nothing.

Patterson's sales process for selling cash registers gave the American economy a tremendous boost. His sales training and motivation ideas were quickly adapted with great success by General Motors, Chrysler, Burroughs, Coca-Cola, Addressograph-Multigraph, Toledo Scale, and many others. Since Patterson's sales manager was Thomas Watson Sr., it is not too far-fetched to assume that without Patterson's effective sales process training, IBM might not exist today.

The history of any successful American company shows that business growth is always the result of a sustained, systematic, and professional sales effort.

3

THE AMAZING
JOHN HENRY PATTERSON

In 1893, while attending the World's Fair in Chicago, John Henry Patterson, the founder of NCR, stopped off at the NCR booth and quizzed the young salespeople about the new cash register models on display. To his astonishment, although NCR had distributed a very comprehensive sales manual to every one of their salespeople prior to the show, hardly any of them knew their product. Patterson promptly hauled the salespeople off to a hotel room for a complete review of their entire product line. The sales staff was so delighted with this meeting that Patterson decided to train all of his salespeople.

In the early sales-training schools conducted by NCR (the first was conducted on April 4th, 1894, in Dayton,

Ohio), the instructors coached salespeople on Patterson's modern concept of thinking in terms of the prospect's needs rather than in terms of the product. Patterson concluded that one-half of all lost sales could be attributed to salespeople's failure to communicate. Patterson taught salespeople to listen to their prospects before launching into a presentation. He showed them how to enhance their presentations on a pad, with graphs to illustrate their selling points in a more compelling way. His instructors conducted practice drills for handling such important customer objections as "Our business has done well without a cash register; we don't need one now."

To combat competition, Patterson even appointed himself head of the "Knockout Department." He kept salespeople informed of the special features of the competitor's machines. However, he told them never to knock their competition in front of the customer: "It pays not to start in on the competitor's defects, but simply prove to the store owner the advantages of our machines."

While Patterson's training offered substance—he aimed at improving professional skills—his competition ignored the value of training and limited sales advice to merely describing basic product features.

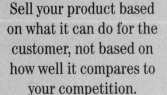

ACTION TIP

Sell your product based on what it can do for the customer, not based on how well it compares to your competition.

Soon, Patterson expanded his sales success beyond the United States. He opened sales offices in Germany, France, Spain, Italy, and South America. Traveling to foreign countries at the turn of the century was expensive and troublesome. In 1896 Patterson set a travel record by visiting 50 cities in 15 countries within 60 days. It would be 10 years later before an American president ever visited a foreign country while in office—the first presidential visit abroad was Theodore Roosevelt's trip to Panama in 1906.

Patterson's improvements did not stop with selling. He knew the relationship between good health and productivity. He banned smoking in his factories, created a country club for employees, installed a 4,500-book library, provided hot lunches, offered movies at lunch time, and instructed all "ladies in our employ" to get 20 minutes of exercise and rest every day. Male employees could use a completely equipped gym and exercise daily with weights. He also employed a staff doctor, nurses, a masseur, and several shoeshine boys. He developed one of the most successful and admired companies in America.

Through his ongoing commitment to improve sales by developing and training people, Patterson transformed the fading image of the Yankee Peddler into the honored profession of selling. Anyone who wants to take a look at the future of selling should take a hard look at John Henry Patterson, the inventor of sales training and the father of "professional" selling.

4

HOW DO YOU EXPAND
YOUR KNOWLEDGE?

Ralph Waldo Emerson once asked, "What is the hardest task in the world?" After a long search for the answer, he concluded that thinking topped the list. What influences our thinking is knowledge. The trouble is that knowledge expands at a much faster rate than our capacity to learn. In the year 1300, the famous Sorbonne library in Paris, France, stored most of mankind's knowledge in 1,338 books all painstakingly written by hand. A diligent scholar could read all of these books in a lifetime and claim to be familiar with the world's knowledge. The steady advances of the human mind and the invention of the printing press expanded book knowledge beyond the capacity of people to absorb the world's wisdom. By 1550, even the best-educated minds would only master 80 percent of their chosen fields and a small fraction of what was known in other disciplines.

Only 120 years later, the German philosopher Wilhelm Leibnitz realized that it was no longer possible to know everything about a single branch of science. In 1670, the Oxford University library in England had swollen to 25,000 books. Even the world's fastest study would have known only about 5 percent of the world's published knowledge after 40 years of reading.

In 1858, Ralph Waldo Emerson wrote that the number of printed books in the Imperial Library of Paris had grown to more than 800,000 volumes. Emerson estimated the annual increase of books to be more than 12,000 per year. Emerson was regarded by many as a genius in his own time; however, he was unable to read more than 2,000 books during his lifetime, less than one quarter of one percent of mankind's accumulated wisdom.

Today, the Library of Congress in Washington, D.C., stores more than 18 million books. The library houses 120 million items (maps, photographs, recordings, and manuscripts) on approximately 530 miles of bookshelves. Yet this huge library contains only a small fraction of the world's knowledge. Given the sheer infinite amount of knowledge, we have to carefully navigate through the maze of knowledge and focus our efforts only on those subjects that help us advance.

Someone once said that if

> SUCCESS PRINCIPLE
>
> The depth of our knowledge determines the quality of our ideas as well as the level of our ignorance.

we drew a large circle on a piece of paper and placed a tiny dot in the middle, the large circle would represent the world's knowledge and the dot what we could learn in a lifetime. If we would quadruple our capacity to learn and read, all we'd do is increase the circumference of our ignorance.

How should we expand our knowledge so we can add value to our lives? Like the traveler consults a roadmap, the seeker of knowledge studies the available choices. What's more important to study: the life of business or the business of life? Is it better to learn the art of living or the discipline it takes to accumulate wealth? Is it preferable to examine the wisdom of the ages or to learn how to age wisely?

Whatever subject we choose, the acquisition of knowledge creates a marvelous by-product: new thoughts. New thoughts create new ideas. New ideas lead to progress. It does not matter how many books we read during a lifetime, but rather how open our minds are when we encounter new ideas. The measure of our progress does not depend on the acquisition of knowledge. Knowledge depends on experience to ferment into wisdom. After all, knowledge without experience is just data. In the final analysis, the measure of a successful life does not depend on how many years we lived, but how we lived our lives.

5

SELLING IS NOT A PLACE FOR AMATEURS

Professionalism in selling has become a hot subject in the top executive suites of America's leading companies. There are three reasons: (1) Global competition demands higher quality products and higher quality relationships; (2) increased professionalism can reduce costly personnel turnover; (3) customers buy more from professional salespeople. According to the U.S. Department of Labor, there are more than 16 million salespeople in this country. Yet in the eyes of leading sales executives, perhaps only one in 10 can be considered a true professional. Although amateurs and professionals may look alike in appearance and grooming, there are significant differences in the way they deal with their customers.

While amateurs tend to talk at the prospect, professionals listen to the prospect. Amateurs are preoccupied with price and discounts; professionals focus on customer requirements and cost-justified solutions. While amateurs leave loose ends, professionals follow up, return calls, and deliver more than they promise.

Amateurs tend to haggle over who will get the bigger slice of the pie; professionals work with the customer to find solutions that create more pie for everyone. In short, the professional salesperson is a trusted advisor who creates a win/win relationship based on competence, integrity, and mutual respect.

There are even more significant differences between amateurs and professionals when we examine their career paths in sales. While amateurs are capable of landing a big sale, their sales charts lack the sustained growth of the professional.

Amateurs tend to hop from job to job without improving their earning power; professionals seize opportunities for learning and growing within their company or their industry. Their income grows at the same steady pace as their experience in the field. While millions of amateurs pay the price of mediocrity, hundreds of thousands of sales professionals earn a very good living and find a great deal of satisfaction in their careers.

Many amateur salespeople fail to become professionals because their real career interests lie elsewhere. Just within the last two weeks I talked to a printing saleswoman who'd rather teach ballet, a software salesman hatching plans for becoming an antique dealer, and a leasing agent with dreams of becoming a writer. All these salespeople would rather be doing something "better" than selling. The sad truth is that none of them is a professional at selling or at anything else.

ACTION TIP

Set aside two hours every week for professional development. In three years you'll be far ahead of your competition.

By now you're probably asking yourself, "How can I move beyond amateur status?" It begins with a commitment to professionalism. Once you've made that decision, you can focus your energies on developing your professional skills and knowledge. Take a closer look at the sales courses offered by your local community college, your industry association, your company, or professional sales training organizations.

Industry associations are now offering certification programs for salespeople, but certification is not limited to salespeople. Even sales managers and marketing managers are beginning to pursue certification. Many universities are now offering degrees in professional selling.

People tend to confuse the terms occupation and profession. Both involve work, but if you don't approach your work with a professional attitude, you can't expect to be successful. Professionalism requires a lifelong commitment to ongoing learning and offers as rewards personal satisfaction and attractive earnings.

6

CUSTOMER SATISFACTION
STARTS WITH THE CEO

With the advent of global competition, selling has become a true profession. More and more universities teach professional selling, and more and more organizations provide certification for sales professionals. Over the past decade, selling in many Fortune 500 companies has shifted away from manipulating the client, and more companies are training their salespeople to become customer focused. Customer-centered selling is the new watchword. Companies have learned that sincere concern about the customer's problems, needs, and goals generates trust and repeat business.

Here are the two big questions: What's the best sales

approach? and Who is really responsible for poor sales practices?

The first answer is easy: The best sales approach is the one that gives the customer the most satisfaction and the salesperson the highest rewards. The second question is more interesting, because good sales practices are a reflection of a healthy corporate culture. Salespeople who work in a culture that does not nurture the individual are more likely to bend the rules and burn bridges, and they won't stop talking about themselves and what they like. A healthy sales culture begins with a CEO who says, "I want my salespeople to be problem solvers; I want them to listen to our customers; I want our back-office team to help salespeople eliminate the hurdles to buying."

It's really quite simple. People pursue what they value most. If a company has high standards, salespeople will go the high road, and they will be genuine, caring, and customer-focused individuals. Sales training in that company will emphasize the human dimension in selling. A clear edict from the CEO will evoke the themes of caring, nurturing, and growing. Why? Because it's good for the bottom line. The question of whether good salespeople are born or trained is a trick question. There is no "born" surgeon and there is no "born" computer programmer. Good salespeople are well trained and, given the

ACTION TIP

Get your CEO involved in the development of large accounts. If the CEO doesn't like to get involved in selling, large customers are not likely to get involved with your company.

right corporate value system, they can make a significant difference in the lives of their customers.

Who is to blame if a customer is not happy with the salesperson? I would not throw the first stone in the direction of the salesperson, but in the direction of the CEO. Good CEOs know that the frontline salesperson represents the entire company. That's why smart CEOs encourage a healthy sales culture. *Selling Power* has interviewed many CEOs who made it a habit to personally take calls from customers, who get involved in the training and motivation of the sales team, and who continually get in front of the troops and listen to the problems salespeople encounter. A good general gives the troops credit for winning the war and takes the blame for losing it; a good CEO gives the sales team the credit for achieving record sales and takes the blame when customers are dissatisfied.

7

MAKE CHANGE YOUR ALLY

Change as a powerful competitive weapon is often ig-nored in well-established sales organizations. Michael Dell, the founder of Dell Computers, once told me, "We be-lieve that if we can't outchange our competition we're going to lose. Look at IBM; they didn't change. They've been very rigid for years, and that's the reason why they've had so many difficulties.

We've created a corporate environment where change is viewed as good. We believe that what was good enough yes-terday is not good enough today. Our senior management is out front each day telling everyone that we've got to do everything better. If you can change and improve better

> **SUCCESS PRINCIPLE**
> The choice is yours: You can take the lead and proactively change or stay in place while change moves you farther from the lead.

than your competition, you will be the world leader in your field."

Anybody who has managed salespeople for a few years knows that telling people to change is one thing, but getting them to change is quite another.

Many salespeople who fear change actually will fight it. Why? They don't recognize the opportunities for change, and they ignore the dangers of not changing. They also are unaware of how to change. If you want to be a positive change agent in your organization, better begin by teaching your salespeople how to change.

Charles LaMantia, CEO of Arthur D. Little, suggests that learning to change is the hardest task for any executive. He wrote, "The key word here is *learning*. Not just learning to manage a one-time improvement effort, but learning to see all your efforts as improvement efforts—and learning to continually improve those improvement efforts themselves, across the entire organization."

This brings up an important question: Is your goal to improve through change, or is it to improve on your improvements?

Let's take sales training as an example. If your goal is to improve, you might add a better speaker to your next sales meeting. If your goal is to improve on your improvement, you might rebuild your entire sales training department. Some sales managers believe in changing as little as possible; others believe in Tom Peters' more radical approach: obliterate and re-create.

How much or how little should you change your sales organization? Look around you. On a scale of 1 to 10 (with 10 being the fastest), how fast do your customers change? How fast do your competitors change? How fast do you change?

If you are a five, and if you rate your customers as a seven and your competitors as a nine, you'd better speed up your change efforts, or you'll end up losing sales, market share, and profits.

David Kearns, former CEO of Xerox, stated that flexibility allows us to be open to change. He explained that inflexible people often stall change through a diligent search for brilliant solutions that never materialize. In an interview with *Selling Power,* Kearns said, "Change is a race without a finish line. In order to make change satisfying, exciting, and nonthreatening, we all must address the critical questions, 'What meaning can we find in change?' and 'What will be the consequences of not changing?' The answers will be the key to change."

8

HOW TO GAIN PERSPECTIVE

The end of the year for many companies means it's crystal ball time, and top managers need to make assumptions about the economy, their company, their competition, and their goals and budgets for the next year. In these turbulent times, it has become difficult to gain a healthy perspective. To gain perspective on things that matter, it may help to understand what "perspective" really means.

Perspective as we know it today has evolved from the architectural drawings of two Italian architects, Brunelleschi and Alberti, who lived in Florence, Italy, in the early 1400s. These noted architects developed a practical method of creating the illusion of depth on a flat surface.

SUCCESS PRINCIPLE

Successful salespeople understand the realities of doing business from the company's perspective as well as from the customer's perspective. They act as ambassadors to help their customers forge successful relationships with their companies.

To understand perspective, we need to understand a few of its essential elements. The first is our vantage point, or the fixed point from which we view a scene. Second is our horizon line, or the point at which the land meets the sky. For example, if we go up in a helicopter, the horizon line gets pushed back and we begin to see more ground and less sky. Third, the vanishing point is a point where lines that are parallel to one another appear to meet at the horizon line. For example, railroad tracks appear to meet at one point at the horizon.

What's interesting about perspective is that it allows us to create the illusion of depth on a flat piece of paper. What's even more interesting is that the rules of perspective also apply to our vision of the world and how we translate this vision into a set of rules for dealing with the world. Here are a few examples.

1. **A single vantage point limits our understanding of the world.** Objects appear very different when we view them from a different position. The moment we move from our vantage point, everything changes. That's why people who don't move mentally have difficulties imagining new possibilities. They can see life only from their point of view, and they can't see new challenges.

2. **Without a horizon line our images become distorted.** As we look into the future from multiple vantage points, we often ignore the horizon line and make mountains out of molehills. Fear tends to magnify difficulties and often prevents us from seeing opportunities. Fear always shrinks the panorama of possibilities.

3. **Imagination influences our perspective.** To see things as they are, we must open our eyes. To see things as better than they are, we must close our eyes. People who accept the horizon line as their natural boundary will never go far. In companies where employees are encouraged to imagine and to build a more successful company, greater profits become the norm, not the exception.

4. **All horizon lines are artificial limitations.** Schopenhauer once said, "Every man takes the limits of his own field of vision for the limits of the world." Whether we see next year as a boom or a bust year does not matter. What matters is that our horizon line will shape the future of our business. A business will always grow at the same rate that the visionary leaders push back the artificial horizon for all employees.

THE FOUR C'S OF MANAGEMENT

I recently read in a science magazine that in the diamond-mining business about 21 tons of rock must be processed to produce one ounce of raw diamonds. It reminded me how challenging it is to move obstacles out of the way before we can achieve shining success. Although most sales managers believe in setting goals, mapping out a sales process, and training, educating, and motivating their teams, the road to success tends to get covered with rocks that need to be shoveled out of the way. In the diamond business, shoveling rocks is merely the beginning: It leads only to raw diamonds. The real work, the cutting and polishing, is a more delicate task. The final work—the delicate handwork—determines the grade of each diamond.

Every sales management task is like mining for diamonds. First comes the spadework, the removal of obstacles, and second, the real job. For example, when a sales manager creates a plan for implementing a CRM solution, or a new e-learning strategy, it will take many meetings and months of thinking and planning before the real job can begin.

The value of diamonds depends on the four C's—clarity, carat, cut, and color. The value of a sales manager depends first on clarity of vision and second on the number of carats, or the weight of the manager's wisdom—the more wisdom and insight the sales manager can offer, the higher the appraised value. Third comes the cut, the manager's ability to shape all facets of a sales team to a level that makes everybody shine. When a diamond is cut to proper proportions, light is reflected from one facet to another and then dispersed through the top of the stone. When a sales team is well managed, all members of the team deliver a shining performance, which enhances the bottom line of the business.

The fourth dimension is the color of the sales manager's allegiance to the team. The best diamonds have no color, and they allow light to be reflected and dispersed as a bright rainbow of colors. The best sales managers bring out the best in their teams and yet don't take credit for their teams' successes.

The "diamond in the rough" is the manager who has a hard time accepting that it takes a lot of hard work to remove obstacles, to cut to the essence of a task, to polish an idea to a level that it creates sparks in everyone's eyes. Some managers get so frustrated with removing obstacles that they don't realize their frustrations turn into flaws, like a diamond's natural inclusions, that lower its market value.

REMINDER

If you want to shine like a star you must bring sunshine to others.

What makes a good manager is similar to what makes a good diamond. While three of the four C's that make up the value of a diamond are dictated by nature, humans control only one—the cut. The goal of the diamond cutter is to maximize the amount of light reflected, not to divert or obscure it. The goal of the manager is no different.

$$\boxed{10}$$

THE TRIANGLE OF
SALES SUCCESS

Many sales managers believe that solid product knowledge is the foundation of sales success. To sell well, the theory goes, salespeople need to develop a detailed knowledge of their product, their markets, and their customers. It's a useful theory, but if knowledge alone were enough to succeed in selling, engineers would be the best salespeople. And they aren't. Many sales trainers believe that to succeed in sales, salespeople need more than knowledge: They need to develop professional skills such as prospecting skills, listening skills, presentation skills, negotiation skills, closing skills, and follow-up skills. It's true. Professional skills help close more sales. But experience tells us that there are many salespeople who are very knowledgeable and highly

> **SUCCESS PRINCIPLE**
> Knowledge creates confidence, skill creates opportunities, and motivation creates winners.

skilled yet never break sales records.

If knowledge and skills together still are not enough to create success in selling, what's missing?

Motivation is the third leg in the triangle of success. It is the desire to win, the ability to bounce back after a setback, and the ability to maintain a positive outlook in the face of adversity.

The goal of a successful sales manager is to help each salesperson on the team to expand the triangle of success.

If you are a sales manager, think of your salespeople. How would you rate them on a scale from one to ten, with ten being the highest level of knowledge, skills, and motivation? Are your salespeople threes, fives, or tens?

In the ideal situation, all salespeople would be tens. Ideally, they are all well-trained, knowledgeable, and motivated. In reality, many of them don't keep up with product knowledge. In reality, many may use skills and techniques that are outdated, wondering why they don't get better results. In reality, many may boast that they are bent on winning, yet in private they admit feeling overwhelmed to the point that they are unable to put in an eight-hour day.

After a sober reality check, let's take a look at the future. If your salespeople are fives today, and they were fives last year, how do you expect them to increase sales next year? If your salespeople are average, your sales results are likely to remain average.

Now, let's take a look at your prospects. Would you call them average or above average in terms of education, skills, and motivation? If your salespeople are calling on high-level decision makers who control important budgets, then these clients are tens, not fives. What will happen when a salesperson that you know is a five calls on a customer that you know is a ten? Right! No sale. Tens like to buy from tens. Just getting an appointment with a ten seems like an insurmountable challenge to a five.

Finally, take a look at your competition. What will happen to your market share if your competitors train, educate, and motivate their salespeople to be tens? Guess who will be winning clients and who will be losing clients? The answer is obvious: A sales force with more knowledge, with better skills, and with a higher level of motivation is destined to win.

11

TEAMWORK MAKES DREAMS WORK

G eneral Norman Schwarzkopf once told *Selling Power* that people come to work to win, not to lose. Yet, for some reason, many teams fail. Why? These teams have been unable to assemble the foundation that supports success. Here are eight key building blocks.

1. **Vision.** Successful teams develop a vision based on a realistic assessment of the opportunity in the marketplace and a down-to-earth appraisal of the team's true capabilities. The purpose of the team vision is to stretch team capabilities, to energize the team's dream, and to boost individual performance.

2. **Commitment.** Basketball coach Pat Riley once said, "The disease of me prevents the evolution of us." A healthy team ego emerges when all team members are 100 percent committed to helping each other win.

3. **Communication.** Teams need a fast and efficient communication system to function properly. The best teams in today's business environment aggressively pursue knowledge and share every bit of information fast, freely, and enthusiastically. The best business teams use the best communications technology.

4. **Interdependence.** At the core of a winning team is trust. Smart teams learn that all team members are part of an ecosystem that is capable of sustaining everyone. Over time, teams realize that each team member has the capacity to contaminate the entire system, but also, that each team member has the ability to cleanse and restore the ecosystem.

5. **Creativity.** To win, every team must solve problems and overcome tough challenges. Studies show that a good team is a lot smarter than any individual alone—providing the team has a methodology for tapping individual creativity.

6. **Diversity.** Teams survive on similarity, but they thrive on diversity. Diversity challenges team members to drop their "diversity bias" and open their eyes to a richer database of experiences and approaches to problem solving.

ACTION TIP

If you want to be part of a great team, leave your ego at the door and help others achieve more.

7. **Care.** Coach Lou Holtz once told his team, "Believe that if enough people care we'll win." The secret to winning for Holtz boils down to a three-part formula: Do right, do your best, and care about others.

8. **Choice.** Every team member has a choice: to play to win as a team or to lose individually. Not every team member can make that choice, and not every team member can win. Building and maintaining a winning team spirit is a formidable challenge. Tough competition mandates that we stand united, tough, and committed, or risk failure.

$$\boxed{12}$$

HOW DO YOU CREATE TRUST?

A recent Gallup poll on public trust shows that we don't trust anyone 100 percent. Americans give the military only a 64 percent trust rating; the police earned 58 percent; and religion is in third place with a 57 percent trust factor. Among the professions, the highest trust ratings went to pharmacists, individual clergy, doctors, dentists, engineers, and college professors. The survey also stated that clergy are trusted more than twice as much as journalists—who, in turn, are twice as trusted as lawmakers. While a code of ethics often specifies what people ought not to do, the creation of trust depends on what people actually do.

To measure the credibility gap in corporate America, the Ethics Officer Association and the American Society of

Chartered Life Underwriters & Chartered Financial Consultants sponsored a survey of 1,324 randomly selected workers, managers, and executives in a variety of industries. The survey found that 48 percent of the respondents admitted to taking unethical or illegal actions in the past year. Fifty-seven percent said that they felt more pressure to be unethical than they had felt five years ago.

In a recent anonymous survey of 255 IS professionals in *Computerworld* magazine, 47 percent admitted to copying commercial software without authorization. Yet 78 percent of all respondents agreed that it should never be done.

Trustworthiness is the backbone of good management. Effective leaders can build trust by encouraging people to rally behind the idea that their work should be dedicated to the common good.

To survive and grow, a company needs to create trustworthiness in the eyes of stockholders, employees, and customers. Sales leaders can influence the level of trust between salespeople and customers, between back office and sales office, and between sales team and management. Creating trust is a far greater challenge than developing a new marketing campaign. Trust demands that the heart, mind, and soul are involved in a full circle that connects all relationships, internal and external. Winning companies forge a supply chain of trust that links their company with the cus-

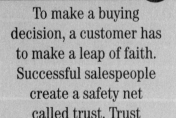

REMINDER

To make a buying decision, a customer has to make a leap of faith. Successful salespeople create a safety net called trust. Trust helps your customers take that leap in complete confidence.

tomer organization. Winning companies know that trustworthiness is equally important to everyone—the employee, the manager, the supplier, the customer, the stockholder, and the community at large.

Trust is not a question of walking the talk from 9 to 5; it demands vigilance around the clock. Trust isn't what we do on American soil, under American law; but it's what we do around the globe. Trust isn't what we say when someone is listening; trust depends on what we do when nobody is watching. Trust is a matter of 360 degrees.

13

HOW MARINES MOTIVATE THE FRONT LINE

I recently visited with a VP of sales of a successful company who is a former U.S. Marine. When he introduced me to his staff, I noticed that many of his top sales producers had been Marines or graduates of the Naval Academy. When I asked him about his recruiting strategy he said, "These recruits have a common value system, they understand what it means to have a mission, and they take pride in everything they do." While former Marine Corps members often run successful sales organizations, experienced business executives are frequently unaware of the motivational master plan that runs America's finest military organization.

Don Carrison, a former Marine and co-author of the book *Semper Fi: Business Leadership the Marine Corps Way,* says sales leaders can learn a lot from the Marine Corps' model about how to recruit the best people, design better training, develop teamwork, inspire loyalty, and achieve victory.

Here are some of the key components of the Marine Corps' blueprint for success:

1. **Recruiting.** Marines send out their top performers to recruit the best people. These experienced officers display a missionary zeal, and they personify the values and pride of a Marine. Carrison suggests that sales managers send out star performers who embody the values of the organization to serve as role models for new recruits.

2. **Training.** Marines spend 12 weeks in basic training. When the training gets tough, drill sergeants often quote the old saying, "The more you sweat in peace, the less you bleed in war." Boot camp is not designed to weed out certain people, but to cultivate everybody. While corporate America fires those who don't perform up to standard, new Marines practice until everybody graduates.

3. **Leadership.** Marine officers lead by example. If a leader asks a platoon to climb a 100-foot wall, he will be the first one to start the climb. Of all military services, the Marine Corp has the highest casualty rate among officers. In corporate America, the best sales managers are not the ones who hide behind their desks, but those who go out to see the toughest cus-

tomers with their front-line people.

4. **Commitment.** The Marine Corps' credo is "Do or die." Carrison says that you have to be careful what you ask a Marine to do because he'll die trying. Marines in action show how much a highly committed team

ACTION TIP

Develop a credo that reflects your core beliefs in dealing with customers. Think about what would happen to your sales if you served your customers as loyally as Marines serve our country.

can accomplish. What if salespeople adopted such high standards for conquering new territories or introducing new products?

5. **Loyalty to the troops.** While corporate America often tells employees that they are replaceable, Marines are told that they are irreplaceable. They know that the entire country and their fellow Marines depend on them. It's natural for a Marine to say, "I love my Marine Corps." How many salespeople say, "I love my company." More and more companies are studying the Marine Corps' model for motivation. As a result, their sales teams take more pride in their product and in their companies. Imagine the possibilities. Imagine every salesperson in your company as proud as a Marine. Imagine how many competitive battles you'd win. Every year, thousands of loyal and highly trained Marines retire: Why not deploy their talents to win more sales?

14

HOW TO ACHIEVE
CONSISTENT SUCCESS

Although there are more than 1,200 books on the subject of success, very few deal with the subject of consistent success. What makes companies like Kellogg, Tiffany, or UPS grow decade after decade, while 80 percent of all new businesses fold within five years? Why do some CEOs stay at the top of their corporations for two decades while others get axed after a few years? Why do some salespeople stay in the top 10 percent year after year while others never reach the top half? Is it destiny that shapes a fixed star and fate that creates a shooting star?

Let's look at what makes businesses consistently successful. Kellogg's founders established a strong value system

> **SUCCESS PRINCIPLE**
>
> In the universe of success, there are shooting stars and shining stars. While shooting stars burn their substance, shining stars share their radiance forever with the entire universe.

based on delivering healthy and wholesome products to their customers. The Kellogg philosophy was simple, it was straightforward, and it captured the imagination of generations of CEOs. As a result, the structure of Kellogg grew consistently while the operation improved consistently, along with sales and profits. The story of UPS follows a similar pattern, and Tiffany has been a jewel of a company since 1837.

Here is a short list of attributes of consistently successful companies and their visionary leaders:

1. **Strong core values are the starting place where all success begins.** We all can choose a philosophy of how to live, work, and succeed. Our chances for success will improve if we consciously define what we want to get out of life and what we plan to give back to society.

2. **Develop crystal-clear focus on a life goal or mission.** Successful people know that new information tends to erode existing knowledge, and old knowledge often interferes with understanding new information. Keep your goals safe from erosion over time. Create a safe place in your mind where all personal-development ideas converge.

3. **Become the architect of a consistently successful life.** Consistently successful people are at the

same time the builders and the architects of their lives. Architects create blueprints; consistently successful people develop life-design strategies.

4. **Manage career decisions wisely.** All careers involve a series of takeoffs and landings. The past 10 years have turned into a decade of downsizing when middle managers have experienced rough landings. Individuals can no longer depend on organizations to provide consistent opportunities for success. People have to think about creating their own structure and design their lives around their own needs, talents, and capabilities. You may find more success by digging deeper right where you are than by taking your spade across the street.

5. **Be more persistent and become more consistent.** There is a difference between having a good time and having a good life. A lucky lottery ticket can make you a millionaire overnight, but it won't make you a consistently successful person. Think of a consistently successful life as a near perfect golf swing. Consistently successful golfers practice every day, year after year, decade after decade. Daily practice ensures your membership in the exclusive club of consistently successful people.

Think about your current level of success. How can you expand on it? How can you make your success last longer? How can you avoid downward career trends? Do you have a life-design strategy? Consider your possibilities. It is your life.

15

AN URGENT REMINDER— THINK PROFITS!

A recent study reports that profits at America's top 1,000 companies fell dramatically during the past year. This drop has turned into unlucky news for millions of executives across the country. Here is a sampling of changes as a result of this decline:

1. Nervous investors are demanding that CEOs no longer assume the job of a chairman and are urging corporate boards to assign the chairman's role to an outsider. Lower profits mean lower job security for CEOs, lower compensation and fewer perks for top executives.

2. Nervous CEOs are drawing up massive restructuring plans, cutting budgets, bonuses, inventory, travel, payroll, advertising, suppliers, and above all, unprofitable divisions.

3. Nervous middle managers are beginning to wear more and more hats, working harder, assuming more responsibility, spending under budget, and squeezing their suppliers even harder than before.

While managers are busy restructuring the company, rewriting budgets, redesigning marketing plans, and reshuffling responsibilities, the real challenge of selling at a profit often gets overlooked.

What can sales executives do to improve profits? Plenty!

1. Spread the word every single day that profitable sales are the only insurance of continued employment. Profit is the lifeblood of your company's future. Profits mean survival and growth opportunities for every member of the company.

2. Put "profit eaters" on a starvation diet. Cut waste, fat, and long-winded discussions. Get more done in less time.

3. Train salespeople to sell price with pride, quote list, and replace the word discount with work that adds real value to the sale. When a customer receives valuable ideas, competent service, and professional treatment, the pressure to discount will melt. Resist demands for discounts by selling the value of your company, testimonials, service, training, appearance, and personal competence in addition to your product. Stop selling price; start selling value.

4. Protect your business against fraud, improper accounting methods, employee theft, kickbacks, and other illegal schemes. Loose ethical guidelines, lax security, and careless supervision cause an ever-widening leak in your shrinking reservoir of profitability.

5. Think productivity. Productivity leads to profits. Ask these productivity questions every day: How can your salespeople meet with more customers every day? How can they close more sales with fewer calls? How can they close higher sales on each call? How can they increase the frequency of repeat sales? How can they work smarter and harder?

6. The best source of profit is excellence. Excellence starts with thinking, continues with action, and ends in superior results. Get salespeople to think before acting. Plan your profits before calling on customers. Think profits before completing the order form, and keep profits by selling your customers on keeping their promises. Set standards of profitability for every salesperson.

REMINDER

In a tough economy 80 percent of all profits are the result of internal decisions, and 20 percent are due to external circumstances. In a great economy, the percentages are reversed.

While pondering the issue of profits, keep in mind that every year more than 60,000 businesses go bankrupt. These businesses lose sight of the fact that the principal objective of a business is to make a profit. Business leaders and sales and marketing executives who overlook their responsibility to keep costs low and sales high will have to make room for those who have a bigger appetite for profits.

16

REVITALIZE YOUR
SALES MESSAGE

What is the number-one problem that stands in the way between you and your prospect? Chances are that your prospects don't know you, your company, or your product; they don't understand your message; and they don't care about your story or your unique selling propositions. Why? Most sales messages fizzle in the marketplace. Back in 1888, very few people had heard of George Eastman and his little black box that he called the "detective camera." Only a few people understood photography, and even fewer knew his company. He started a sales revolution with the simple and compelling message "You push the button, we do the rest."

Since 1888, advances in technology have created a landslide of products and an avalanche of information. Today's customers are bombarded with sales messages that they have learned to tune out faster than ever.

Ask direct marketers and they'll tell you that every year direct-mail response rates decline. Today, more than 99 percent of all direct-mail letters are ignored. Ask sales managers and they'll tell you that up to 90 percent of all prospects ignore a salesperson's attempt to close the sale. Ask yourself how many sales presentations your team made and how many resulted in a sale. Ask marketing managers and they'll explain that 60 percent of all marketing materials are ignored by the salesperson.

Why do most sales messages fizzle? Because we seem to be better at creating new products than we are at creating clear and compelling sales messages.

What makes effective customer messages sizzle? In 1937, the first author to write about selling with sizzle was Elmer Wheeler. His book titled *Tested Sentences That Sell* revealed his experiments with sales messages and their impact on prospects. Wheeler spoke about "meaty words" that prospects could sink their teeth into and "watery words" that had little impact. For example, Wheeler found that if a waiter asked, "Would you care to order a red or white wine with your dinner?" it would double the sales of wine.

ACTION TIP

Don't use boilerplate messages. Your job is to skillfully tease out burning problems during the client interview. The next step is to dress your solution in a tailored sales message that matches the interest level of each decision maker.

Today's customer-message management has less to do with the right choice of products than with the right choice of words. Every market has its own jargon that salespeople need to know. Each prospect lives in a different world that is governed by different preoccupations, perceptions, and preferences. While a CEO's perception focuses on the future, on strategy, and on efficiency, the CFO's preoccupations revolve around cash flow and ROI. For a sales message to gain access to the prospect's mind, it must reflect the language of the market, the preferences of the prospect, and the capabilities of the company.

Unfortunately, very few salespeople are able to translate their company's boilerplate sales message into the prospect's market realities and align it with the prospect's professional preoccupations and corporate challenges.

That's why savvy managers demand that sales and marketing act as a team to create better sales messages. That's why smart companies create sales intelligence centers that can generate customized sales messages by customer category and white papers that are customizable by job title. These companies realize that revitalizing sales begins with a revitalized sales message.

17

CUSTOMER-MESSAGE MANAGEMENT

For many industries, selling in the late '90s was like shooting fish in a barrel. Now the fish are shooting back. The power has gone back to the customer, and a lot of sales managers feel frustrated. It's tougher to see prospects, it takes longer to persuade them, and it's even tougher to close sales. In this uncertain economy only one thing is certain: The old ways of selling and marketing no longer work. As old jokes lose their power from being told too many times, the old sales messages no longer produce the vigorous buying reflexes seasoned salespeople savored because they produced images of laughing all the way to the bank. Here are the key trends from a number of interviews with CEOs, VPs of sales, authors, and consultants.

ACTION TIP

Update and refine your sales message continuously. Your sales, marketing, or advertising team should never be the final judge of what is an effective message and what is not. The only judge is your customer.

1. CEOs are very cautious about the economy. Many have a hunch things may improve, but they are not counting on it. Their mantra is "cost control." A courageous 20 percent of CEOs have stepped up to a higher level of competitiveness. One CEO said, "Business is an unforgiving, relentless, competitive struggle. We're constantly refining our customer message and are expanding our marketing and sales efforts. Those who can't cut the mustard must cut their budgets."

2. **There is a widening gap between sales and marketing.** One of the key conflicts revolves around customer-message management. Marketing is more focused on product facts, while salespeople are more focused on relationships. Salespeople speak the customer's language, but the people responsible for creating marketing materials don't. This often leads to such problems as:

• Marketing messages that are not in sync with real customer concerns.

Experts estimate that 50 percent of a company's marketing material is never used. Top salespeople create their own messages and close sales, while other salespeople miss sales opportunities.

- Marketing messages that don't offer enough substance.

    Today's customers spend a lot more time researching competing solutions and dismiss boilerplate information. When prospects ask questions at a deeper level, salespeople are often unable to differentiate their capabilities or substantiate their claims.

- Marketing messages that are far too complex.

    Customers wonder, "How can I trust them with my problems if they speak about their products in a language that I can't understand?"

Very few companies are able to create a collaborative relationship between sales and marketing that leads to effective customer-message management. CEOs are frustrated because there is so little desire to improve. Said one CEO, "I am always dissatisfied. I preach dissatisfaction. To my mind, everything needs to be improved, or we risk extinction."

Tough times are challenging companies' core missions. Progressive CEOs help recalibrate their core marketing messages to hit the shrinking sweet spots in the marketplace. They boldly redesign their ad messages, refocus their USP, and give their sales teams new tools that capture the hearts and minds of their customers. There is no doubt that the economy rewards those who understand their customers' pain, are capable of offering solutions that work, and above all, speak their customers' language.

18

WHAT'S YOUR STRATEGY FOR SELLING IN TOUGH TIMES?

When the economic pendulum swings toward a recession, sales executives face a series of tough choices. Here are 10 recession-survival strategies that can cushion the rough ride.

1. **Don't put all your eggs into one basket.** Expand your customer base. This is the best time for getting new business because customers are looking for better ideas that can lower costs and increase productivity.

2. **Never be afraid to talk about money early on in the sale.** Don't waste your time with customers who don't have the financial muscle to back up their buy-

ing decisions. Remember, the decision to buy is only the first step of the close. It is better to close two smaller sales than to have one big sale slip away because the customer's financing fell through.

3. **No matter how tough competition gets, never compromise your integrity.** Even when your competition is fighting for sales with dirty tricks, don't lower your ethical standards. If you are in doubt about which course of action to take, get legal advice.

4. **Cut the fat out of your budget, but leave the muscle you need to keep your sales up to speed.** For every hour spent in meetings designed to cut the budget, invest an equal amount of time in thinking of new ways to increase sales. If you look only for ideas for cutting costs, your sales team will never find ideas that could double your sales.

5. **Upgrade your negotiation skills for dealing with collections.** Collect receivables with a carrot and a stick. Sell your customers on the benefits of paying, the troubles saved by sending the check, the advantages of a good credit rating, and the consequences of legal actions. Be friendly, listen to their stories, and no matter what they tell you, always come back with your demands for payment.

6. **Don't go soft when customers try to cancel a firm order.** Tough times will test your sense of fairness. Develop a positive attitude toward the job of "reselling the sold customer." Because of a new budget directive, the customer's boss often will veto a purchase order after it has been signed. Save the sale

by reselling your customer's boss on the benefits of your product and on the necessity to stick with the original agreement.

7. **Selling in a recession is a time of concessions.** Rethink your offer. Can you add extra services? Extra parts? Extended warranties? Deferred payments? Better interest rates? Special options? A longer tryout period? A free loaner in case of breakdown? A free training course for the operator? A factory visit? Can you bundle products together? A three-year, guaranteed buy-back plan? Brainstorm more creative selling ideas today!

8. **Monitor your existing customers' financial health.** Always ask questions about their business plans, their sales, their operating budgets, etc. Learn to look out for the sensitive financial indicators such as payment habits, key supplier payment terms, or bank credits. Remember that bankruptcies always hurt the ones who don't bother to check out red flags.

9. **Don't let the economy depress you.** Although we can't control the economy or our customers, we can control our attitude. Read positive, motivating books, or listen to motivational tapes. Regular exercise is the best antidote against feelings of depression.

10. **Reject the values imposed by those who**

SUCCESS PRINCIPLE

Tough times produce great teachers who challenge us to reach deep within to discover the greatness hidden in our souls.

tell you, "Things will get worse before they get better." People who hold an image of doom in their minds will always pursue a defensive strategy. People who see the silver lining on the horizon will always make the best of the situation and get the business that's out there.

19

A TEN-POINT PLAN FOR SUCCESS

As we prepare for progress in this uncertain economy, one thing is certain: Buyers will ask tougher questions before making a purchase. Here's a list of questions that can help you prepare your sales organization to win.

1. **Do you thrive on change?** If your company's rate of innovation is slower than normal for your industry, you can't expect forward momentum. Customers are always looking for new ideas. If they can't get them from you, they'll get them from your competition.

2. **Are you committed to ongoing improvement?** The more you improve as a company, the better you

can help your customer's business improve. Remember that the more customers improve as a result of your sales efforts, the better your bottom line.

3. **Are you stretching your abilities?** If your salespeople don't stretch their abilities, you'll see a stretch in your company's liabilities. If your team's sales goals are not stretched, your cost of sales soon will be.

4. **Are you removing all barriers to buying?** Companies like Compaq and Dell are able to build and ship a computer within a week. Are you willing to improve your sales performance to a similar world-class level? Do you have a plan for removing all barriers to buying?

5. **Do you exploit new technology aggressively?** The purpose of technology is to save time for the customer, to manage relationships for the sales team, and to help management improve the organization. Is your information technology truly designed to serve people's needs?

6. **Is everyone motivated to win?** People come to work to win, not to lose. Winning demands that the heart be involved in the job. If salespeople love what they do, sales managers will love the results.

7. **Do you measure and reward top performance?** Winners expect results, not excuses. Result seekers are scorekeepers. Set competitive rewards commensurate with the levels of achievement.

8. **Are you managing meaning?** Rethink, resell, and renew your company's mission. If your salespeople

can't answer the question "Why are we doing this?" you cannot expect them to get the job done. Once your sales team knows the "why," the "how" will be easy.

9. **Are you failing forward?** If nobody makes a mistake in your organization, it's a sure sign that you're not growing. Use failure as an opportunity to learn. If you want to triple your success ratio, you have to triple your failure rate.

> **ACTION TIP**
>
> Take a stopwatch, call your own company, and measure how long it takes to buy a product. Then call your two closest competitors and measure their response time. Now rank the three companies. If your company is not number one, work relentlessly to remove the obstacles to buying from your company.

10. **Are you creating trust?** How much trust do your customers place in your company? The answer will be in direct proportion to the amount of repeat business. How much trust do your salespeople place in your company? The answer will be in inverse proportion to your turnover. Do the right thing and you will create more trust.

20

REPLANT TO GROW

It's never easy to understand the time we live in until it's past. Remember the dot-com economy? It was a seller's market, and customers were eager to buy. Even the smallest companies could pick lusciously ripe, low-hanging fruit. How times have changed. Sales have dropped overnight, CEOs have announced layoffs, and CFOs have wielded the budget axe. Today we live in a buyer's market, and sales take an agonizingly long time to close. Salespeople have to make more calls on more decision makers who send out more confusing signals than ever.

In boom times, buyers say yes without much thinking; in a slow-down buyers say no after they've given you their promise. Today a sale is not closed after the customer signs

> **SUCCESS PRINCIPLE**
>
> Whether the economy is great or poor doesn't matter. What matters is how well we appraise the situation and how fast we adapt to change.

the order, but after the check has cleared. That's why some salespeople hold their high-fives until their commission has been paid.

Economic expansions expose structural weaknesses in corporate systems; recessions reveal weaknesses in people. For example, when sales slowed suddenly at Lucent Technologies, the CEO put more pressure on the sales force, the company offered deep discounts, and they flooded sales channels with products. The result: The CEO ordered the VP of sales to retire, the board of directors fired the CEO, the shareholders sued the company, and 10,000 people lost their jobs. Henry Schacht, the new CEO, summed up the costly lesson, saying, "Don't try to run the business faster than it's able to run."

The secret to success, no matter what the economy, is to appraise reality objectively. At the heart of failure is self-deception. In times of great financial success, people confuse capital gains with brains. In times of economic slowdown, people deceive others because they are unable to admit that managers—even those at the top—are vulnerable. They rigidly cling to the illusion that they can single-handedly change the world. A boom makes average performers look brilliant; a recession can make people who took credit for easy pickings look like fools.

The big question is how to adapt equally well in boom times and tough times. Someone once said that there is no such thing as a bad economy, only inadequate preparedness for change. It's all about change and understanding our nature. It's natural to cling to illusions and mourn good times past. But when times change, we must change, go with the flow, and adapt to the new season.

An economic slowdown challenges us to sit down and discover our hidden assets, appreciate our loyal customers, create better ways to serve them, capture new markets, and discover new opportunities. Recessions are the great incubators of new ideas. It's our job to provide the seeds while the economy provides the manure, and if we keep on shoveling and planting, we can make things grow.

21

CUSTOMER RELATIONSHIPS IN A SLOW ECONOMY

The slow economy has companies scrambling to find more-profitable customers. As sales continue to move at a snail's pace, CFOs are pushing budget cuts as a top priority. In the struggle to regain lost ground, many companies make one major mistake: They fail to improve customer relationships. According to Gartner Dataquest, worldwide customer-relationship-management spending on software and services reached $23 billion in 2000. Ideally, this huge investment should deliver greater insight into customers, smoother customer communications, greater customer loyalty, and healthier profits. However, independent research paints a different picture.

Customer satisfaction has not improved. According to a

study by the University of Michigan Business School, between 1994 and 2000 customer satisfaction declined an average of 7.9 percent.

Companies ignore customer behavior. Forrester Research Inc. found that only 23 percent of companies currently improve their online operations by making use of the data associated with how customers use their Websites. A study by Broadbase Software Inc. found that 90 percent of online shoppers click to a competitor's site if they experience poor customer service.

Companies fail to weed out unprofitable customers. According to Newton, Massachusetts–based Meridien Research, 20 percent of a bank's customers generate about 150 percent of unadjusted revenues. At the bottom end, about 30 percent of the customers actually drain 50 percent of the gains realized. But cutting the bottom end without analyzing customer data can backfire. For example, First Union Corporation found that what it had considered the lowest fifth of its customer base in income was actually its most profitable segment.

Companies fail to boost customer loyalty. A customer loyalty study by Deloitte Research showed that when manufacturers set targets for retaining customers and strive to exceed loyalty goals, they are 60 percent more profitable than competitors that don't track customer loyalty well. All that insight had little impact on this year's trend of eroding loyalty. Carlson Marketing Group reported in its annual Relationship Builder survey that in 2000 four in 10 customers showed a genuine commitment to brands or companies. In 2001, that commitment has dropped to just three in 10 customers. Frederick F. Reichheld writes in his book *Loy-*

alty Rules (Harvard Business School Press, 2001), "Outstanding loyalty is the direct result of the words and deeds—the decisions and practices—of committed top executives who have personal integrity." This insight confirms that while CRM technology does not ensure customer loyalty, people do.

> **REMINDER**
>
> When the economy erodes, trust and integrity should not be mistaken for an expendable line item in the budget.

The road to recovery begins with the realization that customer expectations have gone up while the economy has declined. In the dot-com economy customers found it difficult to buy, hence the decline in loyalty. Today buyers make it far more difficult to sell. The message is clear: Sales won't improve until customer relationships improve. It's time to return to such core principles as treating customers well and saying thank you. It's time to return to honesty and integrity. When that happens, customer satisfaction shall again be king.

22

THE ROADBLOCKS TO
SELLING AN IDEA

Recently I spoke with several CEOs that started their own companies. They all agreed that ideas are at the heart of selling. Sound business ideas can come from anywhere. Some people have their epiphany while taking a shower, while others scribble business plans on a cocktail napkin. One woman CEO knew the exact date when the idea for her new company came to her. That idea changed her life. Ideas not only change the lives of those who find them, but also the lives of many other people.

Donald Trump once told *Selling Power,* "There are two kinds of people—those who have good ideas and those who are good at implementing them. Normally, people with good ideas can't implement them, and those who are good at implementing can't produce a single idea."

Most CEOs agree that in order to turn a good idea into a viable business, one has to overcome four major selling challenges.

First, the idea originator must be sure the idea will actually work. Many times the very act of writing down an idea will make it vanish. Most people give up in stage one only to feel a twinge of regret when they realize that someone else is making millions with an idea that they contemplated but failed to complete.

Second, the idea has to be anchored in logic and supported with passion. Logic and emotion are needed to sell the idea to the venture capitalist. Stage two is always a tough challenge for any entrepreneur. The venture capital market is not eager to finance a new idea unless it has a solid chance of succeeding.

Third, the idea must be strong enough to persuade people to join in a collaborative effort to turn the idea into reality. If the original idea fails to capture the imagination of qualified talent, the idea cannot survive.

Fourth, the idea must truly benefit the customer. To keep the selling cycle short, the customer has to understand the benefits quickly. If the idea is too complex for a short and simple presentation, the selling cycle will be too long and the cost of sales too high.

Someone once said that good ideas have many fathers, while bad ideas are always orphans. A good idea fuels progress, creates jobs, increases wealth, and helps advance society. Thomas Jefferson once wrote, "He who receives an idea from me receives instruction himself without lessening mine, as he who lights his taper at mine receives light without darkening me."

Not everyone can move a great idea through all four stages and only the most persistent people will succeed. Is it worth the effort? Ask any successful business leader and they will tell you that a good idea—well conceived and planned and carried through to the creation of a successful company—can truly light up the world.

23

ARE YOU SELLING PROBLEMS
OR SOLUTIONS?

Smart salespeople know that negativity spoils sales. Most daily newspapers don't seem to understand that negative news doesn't sell more newspapers. Think about what you read today in your daily newspaper. Did you find information that you could use to improve your life? Did you read something that would give you a positive feeling? Did you read something that would make you pick up the phone and share with a friend? The truth is that the average newspaper is barely read. As a result, most papers lose subscribers by the thousands, and every month they must spend a huge amount of money to shore up eroding circulation.

A number of recent studies indicate that Americans are tired of picking up newspapers that are overloaded with negative news, cynical reporting, and highly distorted images of the real world. For example, research conducted by the Times Mirror Center for the People and the Press found that 71 percent of Americans think the press "gets in the way of society solving its problems."

Poor journalists have a lot in common with poor salespeople. While poor salespeople tend to believe that they can make the sale if they exaggerate the positive side of their product, poor journalists tend to believe that they can impress their customers if they exaggerate the negative side of the news. It is sad that both the poor journalist and the poor salesperson are completely unaware of how their professional malpractice affects their customers.

Kathleen Hall Jamieson, director of the Annenberg School for Communication at the University of Pennsylvania, was quoted in *The New York Times* as saying, "If you cover the world cynically and assume that everybody is Machiavellian and motivated by their own self-interest, you invite your readers to reject journalism as a mode of communication because it must be cynical, too."

It does not take a Gallup Poll to know that there are more Americans looking for solutions than Americans looking for problems. Ask yourself: What is the ratio of problems to solutions in your daily newspaper? Ten to one? A hundred to one? The truth is most readers have enough problems to handle in a 24-hour period. People all over America want practical, can-do information that they can use to build positive and productive lives. But they can't find it in their daily papers.

Newspaper editors need to realize that balanced reporting means balancing the negative side of the news with constructive articles that deliver solutions, hope, and encouragement. Good salespeople

ACTION TIP

Find out what your customers really need, and fill that need better than anybody else.

are eager to bring more value to their customers. Good journalists could add value to their readers with articles that are free of cynicism by writing stories that offer a constructive, objective, and positive point of view.

It would be interesting to conduct a study that measured the physical changes in people who read a regular newspaper during breakfast and compare it to a group of people who read positive, can-do, solution-oriented information. My guess is that reading the average daily newspaper contributes to indigestion, higher blood pressure, and lower self-esteem. Just think about how a cereal manufacturer would respond if their product caused such a negative reaction? They would immediately recall the cereal, improve the product, conduct more surveys, and thank their customers for giving them a second chance. What do newspaper companies do? They call people while they are eating dinner, trying to sell them a subscription.

24

THE INDOMITABLE *TIMES*

I have always been curious about the mastermind behind *The New York Times*. In 1896, Adolph Ochs took over the reins of the struggling newspaper that, at the time, competed with more than a dozen New York dailies. With a total circulation of only 9,000 copies, Ochs had to move quickly. Fortunately, he was an astute salesman. He lowered the price of the paper from three cents to one penny and promised to publish "the news impartially, without fear or favor." The experts of the day were astounded. Ochs added greater value with better editorial content. He cut out fiction. He cut stale columns. He targeted the paper toward "men in business." He also launched an illustrated Sunday magazine with half-tone photographs and further set himself apart from the competition by heavily advertising the slogan "All the news that's fit to print." By taking the high road in quality and the low road in price, Ochs soon increased the *Times*'s circulation to 350,000.

Arthur Ochs Sulzberger remembers how his grandfather shared his passion for publishing with family members and dinner guests. After dessert he would hand out copies of stories that were to be published in the next morning's paper. He distributed the articles without titles and asked his audience, "What headline would you assign to this story?" After everyone took a stab at it, he proudly revealed the title as it would appear in the paper the next morning.

Arthur Ochs Sulzberger ran *The New York Times* from 1963 until 1997, growing the company from $100 million to $1.7 billion before quietly handing over the reins to his son. When I visited his office, he had a Remington typewriter on one side behind his desk and a computer on the other. I asked him if he used both and he said, "Yes, I learned how to read my email, but when it comes to writing a letter, I use the typewriter." What was the last letter he typed? "Oh, just the other day," he replied with a smile, "I noticed that the front page of the Science section had some problems with the color, so I sent a note to the production manager asking her if we supplied crayons to our readers for that edition."

> **SUCCESS PRINCIPLE**
>
> Success is often measured by the height of a single achievement. Consistent success is only attained by cultivating the same territory longer, better, and more passionately than anybody else.

When people read a story in *The New York Times,* they hardly think about what made it possible for the *Times* to publish 365 issues every year for the past 104 years. That's truly an astounding accomplishment when you think that the high standards Adolph Ochs set back in 1896 still hold today, more than a century later.

The *Times*'s story is the story of a family that has chosen to perpetuate Adolph Ochs' passion for quality with a greater dedication to public service than many other great American families. While such powerful families as the Kennedys reached the limelight through short-lived triumphs and long-remembered tragedies, the Sulzberger family always took pride in perpetuating their product without much bragging. Arthur Sulzberger smiled with self-amusement when he could not remember if his paper had won 78 or 79 Pulitzer Prizes.

The family dynasty behind *The New York Times* is like a great actor who becomes invisible in the portrayal of a character. The Sulzberger family has channeled its energies into the character of the paper. Doing that for more than 100 years—without a lot of fanfare or fighting—that's indomitable character.

25

HOW CAN WE MANAGE THE ZEITGEIST?

I am not an economist, but I have my own theory of what influences financial decisions. And it has nothing to do with anything Alan Greenspan discusses. It's called the *Zeitgeist*. This is a wonderful German word for which there is no English equivalent, but it denotes the collective thoughts and feelings that dominate the era we live in. While the word *Zeit* means time, the word *Geist* has two meanings: One is spirit, the other ghost. Loosely translated it could mean the "spirit of our time" or the "ghost of our time."

For example, the Zeitgeist in the era of Y2K was paranoia about computers crashing on Jan. 1, 2000.

The Zeitgeist of the dot-com boom was marked by euphoria caused by the illusion of growth without limits. It was like a pied piper that invited people to foolishly join in a happy parade celebrating greed.

The Zeitgeist of post-9/11 was like a fire-breathing dragon that attacked at dawn, killed thousands, and vanished into an invisible cave, leaving us behind in a cloud of fear and anger. The Zeitgeist of post-9/11 is marked by severe disappointment. We've paid a heavy price for harboring the illusion that our financial, economic, and military power would make us invulnerable.

It is today's Zeitgeist that influences our decision to stay closer to home, to travel less, to spend more time with our loved ones, to invest in real estate, or to spend a few more seconds looking into another person's eyes. The big question is what changes the Zeitgeist?

History tells us that the pendulum of time keeps swinging. Psychologists tell us that people who suffer disappointment tend to retreat and rediscover their true strength. What feeds the Zeitgeist of our time is fear. What will change the Zeitgeist of our time is courage. It takes a lot of courage to objectively appraise who we really are and what we truly want to get out of life. Upon closer reflection we begin to realize that the Zeitgeist does not really control our lives, we do.

History also tells us that periods of disappointment are always followed by periods when people go back to basics. For CEOs that means trustworthy and responsible leadership. For managers it means that their actions must inspire trust. For salespeople it means more genuine face-to-face contact and more handwritten thank-you notes instead of hastily punched out electronic messages.

Visionary leaders know that the Zeitgeist is really a composite of the past that often ignores future possibilities. While today's Zeitgeist urges us to dwell on the past, we can elude its grip by envisioning a brighter future. Progress demands that we accept the basic insight that's been taught time and again: Our inner strength comes from hope, progress springs from our imagination, and greater meaning comes from building a better future for the generation that follows.

> **SUCCESS PRINCIPLE**
>
> Our progress does not depend so much on understanding the times we live in; it depends more on understanding ourselves and the direction we want to grow in.

Part 2:
Developing into
a Sales Leader

$$\boxed{26}$$

ARE YOU READY TO SOAR?

The dream of flight has captivated mankind for thousands of years. Likewise, the dream of skyrocketing sales appeals to many salespeople. Yet few salespeople turn their dreams into reality. A brief look at the history of aviation provides a blueprint for the steps we can take to turn an idea into reality.

1. **The dream.** About 2,000 years ago, according to Greek legend, Icarus escaped an island prison by creating wings with feathers joined by wax. But he flew too close to the sun, the wax melted, and he crashed into the sea.

ACTION TIP

Like an architect drawing his vision of a building, sketch out your vision of success. Keep that vision in your wallet as a reminder. Many successful businesses were created based on a few basic ideas written on a cocktail napkin.

Question. Are you just dreaming of success? Many people dream big dreams and get excited by possibilities but stop short of taking action. Just this week a salesman told me he dreamed of earning $300,000 within the next five years, but he has no idea how to make it happen.

2. The plan. In 1499, the Italian genius Leonardo da Vinci studied birds in flight and drew sketches of glider planes. He created a detailed drawing of a flying machine that resembled a helicopter. Leonardo da Vinci had great vision, but his immediate environment could not use his plans.

Question. Are you merely planning for your success? Unless your vision is aligned with the capabilities of your team, your best plans will only collect dust. A savvy sales manager once told me, "A plan is only as good as your team's ability to act on it."

3. **The model.** In 1899 the Wright brothers studied the flight of hawks and built their first biplane kite. The glider plane served as the model for developing adjustable wings to control basic flight movements. In December 1903, Orville and Wilbur Wright's motorized plane flew 852 feet and achieved worldwide fame.

Question. Do you launch a new sales plan before making sure it will fly? For example, it is not uncommon for sales managers to purchase notebook computers and off-the-shelf software for their entire sales force without testing it on a small group of salespeople first. Remember, to perform at your best, begin with a successful test.

4. **The space shuttle.** In 1981, the first space shuttle skyrocketed into orbit. To take off, the shuttle's 4.5 million pounds has to defy the law of gravity. With the help of booster rockets, the space shuttle reaches an altitude of 150,000 feet within 120 seconds.

Question. What power will skyrocket your sales? More knowledge? Better skills? Greater motivation? Salespeople often believe that they can skyrocket their sales without a fresh source of energy. Remember, people who succeed go through all four phases: They dream big dreams; they develop realistic plans; they test several possibilities; and they invest as much energy as needed for their sales to take off. Achieving success is not rocket science, but it is only possible if we follow the blueprint from dream to reality.

DO YOU USE THE RIGHT FUEL FOR YOUR ENGINE?

Many salespeople start their careers filled with hope, anticipation, and determination. They are willing to give their very best to reach sales and income goals. After a few years they get used to receiving larger checks and discover they are spending their money faster than ever. One day, these salespeople realize they are driven by the need to meet bigger and bigger monthly payments. Since their spending faucet is wide open, they have to carry bigger buckets to replenish their reservoir. As a result, they feel depleted and often complain about the futility of the "rat race." What caused the shift from reaching for lofty goals to simply hustling for money? What caused the transformation from being open-minded to becoming single-minded?

> **REMINDER**
>
> There is an untapped reservoir of capabilities within each of us that helps us deal with life's toughest challenges. Once we make the effort to dig deeper, the human brain will organize itself to tackle any challenge.

Most important, what happened to the hope, anticipation, and determination that made selling so exciting in the early days? The answer is simple: These salespeople ran out of fuel.

Of course, the human mind does not work like a machine, but just imagine for a moment that it is a special, powerful six-cylinder engine. But unlike a mechanical engine that functions well on one type of fuel, the human engine needs different kinds of fuel in order to achieve its peak potential. Imagine that each one of the six cylinders is connected to its own special fuel reservoir. These six reservoirs fuel the engine of success:

1. **The fuel of higher meaning.** If you dedicate your life to a higher cause than yourself, you will never want to stop contributing. Create enough meaning and you will create enough energy. If you limit the meaning of your work to money, you will soon run out of energy.

2. **The fuel of joy.** Never miss an opportunity to create joy for others. Decide today that it won't hurt you to smile more often or to share a laugh with a client. Life is much more than doing business. If you put more fun into your work, you will get more fun out of your work.

3. **The fuel of leadership.** Seek out good leaders. Allow them to stretch your abilities. Store away their lessons and use them as a fuel reserve to get through tough times.

4. **The fuel of goals.** Goals are the architects of hope. If you run out of goals, all other cylinders will inevitably grind to a halt. Salespeople need to plant hope in the fertile soil of the imagination. Lack of hope inevitably leads to depression.

5. **The fuel of teamwork.** The days of the lone ranger in selling are history. Today's winners are part of a successful team. If you help other people win, you will have a team of people helping you win.

6. **The fuel of rewards.** Enjoy the fruits of success, share the credit with your team, and preserve the lessons you learned from each victory. Maintain an attitude of gratitude. View each peak performance as a refueling stop from which you can launch your next success.

If you find yourself only running on two cylinders, check your reservoirs and replenish them today. It may surprise you, but all the fuel you'll ever need to reach the highest peaks is already stored within you. It's up to you to release the valve that will let it flow.

28

THE VALUE OF CURIOSITY

One day not long ago, at a luncheonette in our small town, an elderly gentleman seemed to be looking for a place to sit. I asked him to join me, and we started talking. He was intensely curious. Within minutes he knew that I was born and raised in Austria, that I started *Selling Power* magazine, and that we have 200,000 subscribers in 67 countries worldwide. Each time he had collected a piece of information, he asked for more. He was genuinely interested, which made it a pleasure for me to answer his questions.

Then, reversing the process, I found out that he had started his career as a car salesman. Later he moved on to real estate, invested in commercial properties, and later developed office buildings and shopping centers. As he told his story, I realized that I was talking to one of Virginia's richest men, whose net worth exceeds $340 million. I was impressed with his humble and modest demeanor. Whenever there was a pause in the conversation, he didn't fill the space by talking more about himself, but continued with questions designed to learn more about *Selling Power.* After we finished our lunch, he asked me to send him a magazine so he could share some selling ideas with his sales manager.

Our conversation made me wonder about the power of curiosity. People who are genuinely curious ask more questions and tend to get more answers. In return they learn more. While many trainers and consultants teach the importance of asking questions and the art of good listening, nobody teaches us how to harness the power of curiosity.

Curiosity moves people from complacency to action. What fuels curiosity? Interesting and deeper questions move people to the outer branches of the ever-growing tree of information. As more new pieces of the puzzle emerge, we feel more compelled to uncover the entire picture. Curiosity leads the mountain climber to higher elevations. Curiosity compels the inventor to think deeper. Without Thomas Edison being curious about finding a filament that would emit light but wouldn't burn up in a vacuum tube, there would be no light bulb. Without Madame Curie wondering about a curious sub-

> **SUCCESS PRINCIPLE**
>
> We live in a world that appears to reward superficiality, but these rewards don't satisfy our souls. Greater rewards go to those who are curious and engaged in the pursuit of meaning.

stance that emitted light when she left it in a petri dish in her laboratory overnight, there would be no X-ray technology.

Curiosity is the most overlooked sales tool. Curious salespeople move from the traditional role of the transaction agent up to the level of a business partner who can help transform the customer's business. Curiosity is the secret to mankind's progress. At one point, the leading scientists of the world thought that the earth was flat and that anyone going to the edge would fall off. People who lack curiosity never bother to expand their horizons. They will never know of the riches waiting for them if they only bother to move outside their comfort zone. Curiosity led my luncheon partner to realize that living outside his comfort zone ensures a far more interesting and dynamic life.

29

THE POWER OF CONCENTRATION

Concentration is one of the most important keys to success. If we tirelessly apply our physical and mental energies to one problem, we will meet with great success. So how can we improve our powers of concentration? Golf champion Arnold Palmer believes that concentration demands good self-knowledge. He explains, "The secret of concentration is the secret of self-discovery. You reach inside yourself to discover your personal resources and what it takes to match them to the challenge."

People who have difficulty concentrating on their jobs often blame others. Brendan Francis argues, "Other people's interruptions of your work are relatively insignificant compared with the countless times you interrupt yourself."

SUCCESS PRINCIPLE

A diamond has the same chemical composition as a hunk of coal, the only difference being that it decided to concentrate a lot longer.

Research shows that with improved concentration comes an increased flow of productive ideas. TV producer Norman Lear told *Selling Power* that there is an infinite flow of creativity we can all tap into, providing we concentrate without forcing the flow. If we are too preoccupied or self-centered, the flow will stop. If we forget ourselves in the task, the creative flow will increase.

Mihaly Csikszentmihalyi (pronounced Chick-SENT-me-hi), professor of human development at the University of Chicago, once described how superachievers concentrate to reach "the zone" of total absorption. He said that anxiety kills the flow, as does boredom. In the same way that an archer pulls the string against the bow to create tension, a superachiever fills the mind with a challenge that causes new ideas to flow with high velocity toward a mental bull's-eye.

Olympic athletes often create a series of ritual steps that help them concentrate on the present moment. Their objective is to forget the preoccupation with success and failure and to focus all mental energies on the challenge at hand.

The success-oriented mind is like a magnifying glass that focuses the rays of the sun in one concentrated spot. The magnified intensity of the rays dissipates the moment the glass is out of focus. When our minds wander from subject to subject, our productivity drops, our energies get sapped, and our motivation dissipates.

Inventor Thomas A. Edison once told a reporter how to use the power of concentration to achieve something of significance. "You do something all day long, don't you? Everyone does. If you get up at 7 o'clock and go to bed at 11, you have put in 16 good hours, and it is certain with most people that they have been doing something all the time. They have been either walking, or reading, or writing, or thinking. The only trouble is that they do it about a great many things, and I do it about one. If they took the time in question and applied it in one direction, to one object, they would succeed. Success is sure to follow such application. The trouble lies in the fact that people do not have an object—one thing—to which they stick, letting all else go."

We can all build a great mental framework in which concentration will flourish. If we apply razor-sharp concentration, there is nothing that can hold us back from winning.

30

HOW LONG DO YOU STAY FOCUSED?

Everybody wants to be successful, but not everyone can find the way to success. Why? I believe that most people simply get lost. Let me explain. Have you ever looked up a word in a dictionary? Your intention may have been to check the definition of a word. You go through the pages alphabetically. Let's say that the word you're looking for is *perspiration*. On the way to the P's you stumble onto the word *orotund* and wonder what it means. You find out that it means *pompous*. Since you're on your way to the P's you glance at *pompous* and find *pretentious*, which leads you to *ostentatious*, and in the process you forget about *perspiration* altogether. The result: lots of sweat, but no progress. The cause: lost in thought.

Let's take another example. Have you ever gone to a grocery store with the intention of getting milk, cereal, and batteries and walked out with 12 or 15 items, but no milk? What prompted you to deviate from the milk aisle and pick up two magazines, cookies, ice cream, mouthwash, and a can of cling peaches? The cause: lost in action.

A third example will drive the point home even more clearly. Have you ever sat down in front of the TV just to relax for a few minutes and found yourself two hours later engrossed in a movie, forgetting that you have a life? The cause: lost in images.

As the world grows in complexity, there are more chances for getting lost in thought, action, and imagination. When we get lost, we're like children on a rocking horse, fully engaged, always in motion but going nowhere.

If we get lost in such simple tasks as shopping, how about more complex tasks such as the pursuit of a large account, the management of a team, or the pursuit of our career?

In order to pursue success, we need to be aware of the impulses that lead us to run in place. The intention of the world is to divert us from building a path to success. Heavyweight boxing champion George Foreman once told *Selling Power* that "Success begins with a decision." If you set your mind to reach a goal, you'll make certain that you reach it. You'll say no to all distractions, detours, and time-wasting activities. As a result, you can clearly focus on reaching your destination without detours. It is the decision to be successful that helps you develop an internal guidance system that keeps you moving upward and onward.

Think about the dreams you had 10 years ago. What happened to them? What about the five-year goal you set five years ago? Where did it go; where did you go? What about today? Where do you want to be by the year 2010? Sylvester Stallone once reflected upon his own success saying, "I am not the smartest or the most talented person in the world, but I succeeded because I kept going and going." Those who go furthest are the ones who stay focused on the decision to pursue their life's mission.

31

FOCUS ON PRODUCTIVITY

Successful people know that lack of steady commitment to staying productive waters down results and leads to wasted time and effort. So why do so many people get pulled off the productivity track? Here are three common causes:

1. **Multitasking.** Achievement-oriented people often tackle two or more tasks at once without doing any task well. You can hear the telltale signs of "multi-tasking" during many phone conversations—an envelope being ripped open, a keyboard clicking, a modem dialing. The caller is reading the morning mail, typing a letter, or checking email.

ACTION TIP

Develop a to-do list before you go to bed each night. You will sleep better and not worry about the amount of unfinished business ahead of you. At the end of the next day you will feel a sense of peace when you cross items off your list and start your to-do list for tomorrow.

2. Opportunity chasing. Often at trade shows a salesperson engages you with a quick smile and answers a few questions. As you study the product, the salesperson is reading the name tags of people standing behind you. At business conventions people often dart around like hunters rather than zeroing in on one prospect, planting seeds and nurturing a relationship like farmers.

3. Brief mental escapes. When you are meeting with a customer, do your thoughts race ahead or drift back to unfinished business?

A noted psychologist, Van Reisdorf, found that unfinished business has a disruptive effect on the mind. A fight in the morning may leave its imprint on our thoughts throughout the day. A canceled sale can negatively impact your attention span on the next call. It can throw your focus into disarray. On the other hand, a focused sales executive can accomplish more in three calls than an unfocused one can in ten. Here are a few suggestions for increasing your ability to focus on productivity.

- Make a decision to live one moment at a time and to think one thought at a time. To clearly focus your thoughts, think of a laser gun, not a shotgun.

- Focus on one person at a time. When you are with a customer, be with that person 100 percent. No other sound or sight should be more important.
- Start with a clean slate. Brush away any mental cobwebs before you meet with your next customer. When you start mentally with a clean slate, you can become a solution provider, but when your thoughts revolve around you, you become the obstacle to a sale.
- Set daily goals. There is no need to pay attention to everything in sight. Instead of watching mindless TV, quietly reflect on your day and set a goal for a more focused and mindful tomorrow. Stop subdividing your focus into fragments. Someone wise has said that the past is to be learned from and not lived in; the future is to be planned for, not paralyzed by; and the present is to be enjoyed right now.

32

WHO CHARTS YOUR SALES PROGRESS?

Both management experts and top salespeople agree that we can only improve what we can measure. Salespeople who keep good records of their sales performance tend to outperform those who depend on others to tell them how they are doing. Top performers know that all sales activities can be measured and the key numbers are all related to one bottom line—the salesperson's earnings. Here are a few key numbers you can use to chart your progress:

1. **Number of high-yield customers.** Top performers classify their customers into A, B, and C accounts. If their database contains 300 contacts, chances are that 20 percent of them are A accounts that produce

SUCCESS PRINCIPLE

Imagine what would happen in a football game if you removed the clock, the yard-lines, and the scoreboard? It would be chaos. Stop working in a chaotic world. Review your sales progress every day, and measure your progress against your goals. You can't break records if you don't keep records.

about 80 percent of their sales. Top salespeople rise to the top because they invest more time with their top accounts.

2. Weekly volume of sales calls. Every salesperson knows that more sales calls will translate to more sales, yet very few keep track of how many customer contacts they make each week. Begin tracking your call volume starting today. As you learn more about how your call volume progresses each day and each week, you will learn more about the obstacles that prevent you from making more calls. Each week set a new call volume goal and challenge yourself to break new records.

3. **Number of new qualified prospects per week.** Prospecting is vital to success. Every week, delete some of the useless names in your database and replace them with an equal or greater number of new, qualified prospects. Set weekly prospecting goals and you will prosper.

4. **Time devoted to "prime-time" activities.** Each day write down the time of your first call and the time of your last call. Next, find the reasons why you started calling late or quit early. Top performers divide their time into "prime time," that is customer calling time, and "paper time" when they write pro-

posals, do research, or catch up on paperwork. If you find yourself planning your day from 9 a.m. to 10 a.m., you're not achieving prime-time productivity.

5. **Competitors' sales results.** Know your competition and monitor their sales results. If you use a contact management program, create contact records and keep track of each competitor's sales. The more you know about your competitors' strategies, the better you'll be prepared to outsell your competition.

In the same way that securities analysts check the financial health of a company by looking at a few key indicators, a sales manager can check the health of a sales territory by reviewing a few key sales ratios: number of good prospects in the database, number of sales calls made per week, ratio of calls to closes, or the number of new prospects entered in the database per month. Only if we look beyond such obvious numbers as sales volume and sales costs can we begin to open our minds to higher levels of performance. Make it a habit to record and visualize your key sales numbers and develop your own scoreboard. Remember, to break records, you have to keep records.

33

THE SELLING POWER OF WORDS

If knowledge truly is power, then words are the arsenal that creates your power base. Vocabulary gives you the power to differentiate ideas. For example, a salesperson who does not recognize the difference between the word *objection* and the word *objectives* can't differentiate between an obstacle and a goal. A sales manager who thinks *salesperson* and *team player* mean the same thing doesn't understand the relationship between power and motivation. A leader who does not see the difference between vision and perception can't be expected to see the forest for the trees or to inspire a team to outsell the competition.

A rich vocabulary gives you the power to recognize and

> **SUCCESS PRINCIPLE**
>
> Carefully chosen words are the salesperson's most precious assets. There is nothing worse for a salesperson than having nothing of value to say.

reconcile differences, to recognize and capture opportunities, and to recognize and find success.

Words can breed fear, reassure, dissuade, or persuade. The right word throws a switch in the mind to steer a person in the right direction, and the wrong word can throw you off course. One misspelled word can prevent FedEx from delivering a package; it can cause a pharmacist to fill the wrong prescription; it can stop a customer from reading a proposal.

Words can change the way people think. Words on paper, written by ordinary citizens, have overthrown governments and changed the course of history.

Words are subject to change, and their power decreases over time. That's why selling messages must keep up with the times. For example, in 1886 Coca-Cola sold with the simple slogan "Drink Coca-Cola." In 1908 it changed to "Sparkling—harmless as water, and crisp as frost." In 1924 it advertised "Pause and refresh yourself." In 1944 it suggested, "How about a Coke?" In 1957 Coke became "the sign of good taste." In the tension-filled 1960s people were encouraged to "Relax with Coke." In the booming '80s Coke proclaimed "Coke is it!" In 1990 consumers heard "Can't beat the real thing." In 1993 it switched to "Always Coca Cola," and by 2005, "Make it real."

In selling and marketing, words are the armory of thought that forge the weapons by which economic battles are won. The right choice and judicious application of words facilitate discovery, increase comprehension, boost persuasion, and lead to greater success.

To succeed in our knowledge-based world, we need to recognize the interdependent elements of a knowledge-based system. Sales success is powered by information. Information is powered by knowledge. Knowledge is powered by words. It's a simple success triangle. Words are like nets that we cast into the sea of information to catch the knowledge we need to survive. Salespeople who fish with fewer words will net fewer accounts and will find their customers washed away with the tide.

34

ARE YOU A TALK-AHOLIC?

W hy do we often talk more than we should? When other people talk too much, we notice immediately. When we talk too much, everyone else notices except us. How many times have you noticed salespeople talking themselves right out of a sale? How many times have you heard the complaint, "When you ask him what time it is, he tells you how to build a watch"?

While good, long talks can enhance relationships, most customers prefer salespeople who are brief and to the point. Why do some people talk too much, and what can we do about it? Here are a few thoughts to ponder.

1. **Anxiety.** People who are anxious use an avalanche of words to avoid dealing with potential conflict (like a prospect saying no). Instead of balancing talking with listening, they believe that their wall of words will protect them from what they imagine as a threat. They often refuse to give up control of the conversation by adding a trail of words that echo the ones that they've expressed previously.

2. **Lack of preparation.** The less clear we are on any given subject, the more words it will take us to talk about the subject. Here is an eye-opening exercise. Ask a salesperson to make a presentation about your company as if you were a new prospect. Time the presentation. Next, ask the salesperson to write a brief, but concise description of your company on one page. Now, read the copy at normal speed. How much time did it take? Much less! The lesson? Lack of preparation stretches the presentation.

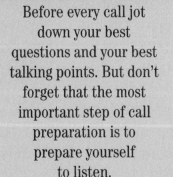

ACTION TIP

Before every call jot down your best questions and your best talking points. But don't forget that the most important step of call preparation is to prepare yourself to listen.

3. **Stress.** When we are tired we tend to ramble, and our ability to concentrate begins to decrease. Our brain responds to mental fatigue by producing more words and less meaning. The cure: Get enough sleep, eat healthy, and exercise regularly.

4. **Lack of a roadmap for your conversation.** Do your salespeople have a road-

map for their sales calls? If not, ask them to write down the answers to three questions: What is my call objective? What information do I need to get? What information do I plan to give? Encourage your salespeople to talk less and listen more.

5. **Lack of a budget for your time.** Some get so involved in conversations that they lose track of time. Budget a specific amount of time for each call and stick to it. If you are a manager and you want to save time, conduct your meeting standing up. This forces people to be brief and to the point. If you meet with longwinded people, remind them five minutes before you plan to leave by saying, "We have another five minutes, what else do we need to cover?"

6. **Lack of humility.** Some people think that everything they say is profound and important. When they talk, they experience a rush of good feelings, and they often fall in love with their own words. Don't be a talk-aholic. Being expressive is nice; however, good relationships require us to be receptive to others.

7. **Ineffective thinking.** While some salespeople continue to hopscotch from problem to problem, others quickly get to the core of a customer's problem, solve it, and close the sale. How? They use two types of thought patterns that can cure talk-aholism: convergent thinking and divergent thinking. While convergent thinking leads to a focal point in the middle of a circle, divergent thinking radiates—like

the sun—away from the center in every direction. Divergent thinking opens people's minds, it leads to new ideas, thoughts, and possibilities. As a result, the conversation goes on and on. Convergent thinking leads to conclusions and concrete results, like a closed sale.

35

WHAT INFLUENCES THE BRAIN OF THE BUYER?

Recent research shows that at the time of birth a baby's brain has only reached 25 percent of its full capacity. Brain scans show that it takes three years for the human brain to develop, provided the infant benefits from a stimulating environment. If stimulation is poor, the brain will not function as well and will show inhibited growth. Babies who receive positive eye contact during feeding, for example, develop fewer vision problems. Researchers found that lack of eye contact between baby and parent can lead to such problems as myopia and even temporary blindness.

The second key component to the growth of the brain is sound. A baby's hearing develops better in an environment that alternates periods of quiet and periods filled with happy sounds. Without this exposure infants may experience such difficulties as speech disorders or hearing loss.

Human touch is another factor critical to brain growth. Researchers at UCLA report that premature babies who are exposed to daily skin-to-skin contact thrive more vigorously and gain weight more quickly than those left alone in an incubator.

In the field of sales and marketing, there have been a number of studies on how the customer's brain gets positively stimulated to grow healthy sales.

Let's take visual stimulation. Images are great selling tools that communicate more content much faster than words. Dr. John Hart of Johns Hopkins University found that it takes only 300 milliseconds for us to identify a picture or an object. The more visually appealing the presentation, the better the chances of selling the customer. Images convey potential reality and start a new thought process in the customer's mind. Prospects who don't "get the picture" won't buy.

Second, salespeople need to sound positive in order to be persuasive. Researchers in the field of psycholinguistics found that customers like to buy from people whose speech patterns come closest to their own. When a customer speaks slowly, it pays to slow your speech to the same volume of words per minute.

Tone of voice is another vital component for building trust and rapport. Dr. Albert Mehrabian of UCLA found that we communicate 38 percent of feelings and attitudes through tone of voice. Salespeople who are able to modulate their voices to "harmonize" with their customers tend to sell more, as do those who listen thoughtfully and use silence strategically during the final moments of the sale.

The third factor involves applying the right human touch to increase trust. The best selling idea in the world won't grow into a sale without intensive preparation, high-

> **REMINDER**
>
> The quality of your relationship with your customer determines the profitability of the account.

touch presentations, quality contacts, and diligent follow up. In much the same way that parents help a baby's brain come to life, a salesperson can implant and grow an idea in the customer's mind and help bring a new sale into the world.

$$\boxed{36}$$

TURN KNOWLEDGE INTO ACTION

Successful sales executives have one important edge over peers who achieve only average results. That edge lies in their ability to turn knowledge into action. Some people know how to talk smart in meetings, but when it comes to action they hesitate, retreat, ponder, or procrastinate. They have knowledge, yet they don't realize they have to take the next step to achieve a goal.

Sales executives who are action oriented show measurable results at the end of the day. Knowledge-focused people will often spend an entire day coming up with reasons why something can't be done. Sometimes smart people don't realize that action is often a greater laboratory for

ACTION TIP

Every Sunday evening, write down your action plan for the week. The reason we don't turn more ideas into action is that our memories are more perishable than our motivations to act.

learning. Without taking action steps, no one ever learns what will work and what won't. Theories never made a sale.

Many companies put a premium on knowledge and are proud of being "learning organizations." The concept of knowledge management is a smart idea. It's a strategy of getting the right information to the right people at the right time, so that they can take action and create value.

Yet, as Starbucks president Howard Behar said, "A learning organization is useless unless it is a doing organization."

In the field of sales management, it is fairly easy to find information on best sales practices; it is far more difficult to get the entire sales team to apply these practices consistently and successfully. There are several forces that stand in the way of getting a sales team to act in a purposeful, focused, and determined fashion.

1. **Uncertainty.** Every time the economy goes through a change, the uncertainty about what comes next increases. Uncertainty is the big pie thrown into the face of knowledge management. Smart sales leaders teach their team that action always requires more courage than knowledge. Without courage there is no chance for success.

2. **Procrastination.** H.W. Shaw once said, "The greatest thief this world has ever produced is procrasti-

nation, and he's still at large." What causes many salespeople to procrastinate is fear. They may fear change, rejection, or failure. When Lance Armstrong was asked how he won the Tour de France seven times in a row, he replied that he did not do it by procrastinating.

3. **Lack of energy.** Salespeople often become energized when they get to perform their favorite task (like demonstrating a brand-new product), but when it comes to writing follow-up proposals they only do the bare minimum. Salespeople who display a lack of energy often work for managers with low expectations.

4. **Lack of leadership.** Very knowledgeable sales leaders often succeed by talking their way into a position of power, but they often fail to inspire their team to tackle the challenges that will move their business to success. Successful leaders encourage their team to take the best course of action, even at the risk of failure. These effective leaders act with purpose, and they are clear about their intentions. They act in concert with their strong beliefs and make sound decisions. President Theodore Roosevelt once said, "I am just an ordinary man without any special abilities, except this: I do the things that I believe ought to be done. And when I make up my mind, I act."

The difference between a company and its competitors is the ability to act and execute quickly. To succeed, it takes fewer people who can "think smart" but more people who can "act smart." You know it. So, just do it.

37

ACT YOUR WAY TO SUCCESS!

Constantin Stanislavski, a world famous director, wrote a well-known book called *An Actor Prepares*. This great book, in addition to being one of the best for the profession of acting, is also a fascinating book for salespeople. Surprisingly the book describes many useful techniques for improving sales performance.

Stanislavski advised actors to add more life to the characters on stage by acting "as if" their imagined role were real. One of his key methods for adding more life to the character lies in the realization that a new role does not need to be the beginning of a new experience, but the continuation or expansion of a past experience.

In other words, the actor can play the new role as if it

> **REMINDER**
>
> Customers are just as capable as salespeople of putting on an act. Relationships improve the moment people decide to drop their masks and deal with one another as authentic human beings.

were a replay of emotions generated by one of his real experiences in the past. Given the tremendous success of this method employed by actors like Robert Redford, Jack Nicholson, or Dustin Hoffman, it can even become a powerful self-management strategy for our thoughts, actions, and feelings in a selling situation. By choosing positive "as if" assumptions, we can influence the outcome of a sales call. Here are a few examples:

1. When you present your product, act "as if" it is the most precious item in the world. For example, Ed McMahon used to sell fountain pens on the boardwalk in Atlantic City long before he became a famous television personality. He learned to hold a fountain pen as if it were a fine piece of jewelry, and he set new sales records in the process. He added more life to his selling performance and more income to his pocketbook.

2. When you meet your next customer, act as if you are enthusiastic, even when you are not. Mary Kay Ash, the founder of a $1 billion cosmetics company, used to tell her sales consultants, "Action creates motivation. If you act enthusiastically, you will soon feel real enthusiasm."

3. Here is another as-if exercise: When you give your next group presentation, act "as if" you were the kindest, most caring, and most confident person in your company. To add more life to this new role, think of your own past experiences when you have felt kind, caring, and confident. Then replay this feeling of success and the sense of confidence in your new role and you will soon become the best salesperson you can be.

Another technique taught by Stanislavski is the "invisible circle." He told actors to imagine an invisible circle around them that protects and shields them from any outside influence. Anyone outside the circle would be subject to the actor's influence, but nobody on the outside could penetrate the actor's invisible, protective shield. That shield creates a powerful feeling of confidence and comfort.

Good acting requires more than surface skills such as striking a pose. Good actors make their art disappear by creating an authentic character from within. Likewise, good salespeople make their art disappear, and as a result of their skills, their customers never feel that they have been "sold."

38

HOW DO YOU REACT
TO FAILURE?

Bob had it happen to him. After 20 years in sales and sales management, his company merged and half his sales staff was eliminated. So was his position. Bob received a generous severance package and took his family on a two-week vacation just to clear his mind about what he wanted to do. Six months later he is still without a job, feeling bitter and blaming his former boss for not warning him about the merger.

Elizabeth met with failure in a different way. After dozens of calls and pages of detailed proposals she landed a large sale that made her eligible for a trip to Hawaii. The day the order was supposed to be shipped, she received an urgent email message from her CFO that the customer had failed to send the down payment. She decided to visit the customer who wrote her a check for the full amount in exchange for immediate shipment. Unfortunately, the check bounced, and two days later the client company went into Chapter 11.

How do you react to reverses of fortune in your sales career? When most people think of a successful career, they often imagine a continuous string of victories, a steady upward movement, and a predictable supply of manageable challenges. In real life, successful people are those who have stumbled, picked themselves up, learned more about themselves, and moved on to tackle even greater challenges.

Research suggests that how we respond to a setback depends on what psychologists call ego strength. Do you seek comfort after failure, or do you seek solutions? How long does it take you to find the best course of remedial action? Do you punish yourself by sticking your head in the sand, or do you accept the situation, hold your head up high, and move on? Do you ignore failure, or do you learn from it? The answers to these questions are determined by our ability to appraise reality objectively, which is the hallmark of ego strength.

Ego strength divides executives into three types:

1. **The Sherman Tank.** These sales executives have armored their egos with steel plates. Like bullets that ricochet off a Sherman Tank, failures just bounce off their egos without leaving a scratch. They forge ahead in the face of failure, either denying it or pretending that nothing happened. Sherman Tanks

believe that denial or cover-ups are effective coping strategies. The downside of their rigid strategy is twofold: They never learn from their failures, and they are very vulnerable when failures hit too close to home.

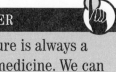

REMINDER

Failure is always a bitter medicine. We can either swallow the medicine so it can release its power, or refuse to take it and fail again.

2. **The four-wheel drive.** These sales executives have the greatest ego strength. When they run into the ruts of failure, they shift gears, apply a greater torque on all four wheels, and roll on. Although they experience the sting of failure, they don't allow their egos to get bent out of shape. Four-wheel drives have faith in their ability to accept failure, they know how to manage adversity, and they have the courage and faith to survive disasters.

3. **The convertible.** These executives see failure as an opportunity to open up. When adversity hits, they don't hide; they closely survey their surroundings. In the process they discover more about what influences them and how they can build on their strengths. When adversity strikes, convertible executives respond with openness, leading to more realistic worldviews. They see failure as an opportunity to become more humble, more accepting of other people, and more focused on what really matters.

39

HOW TO TURN SETBACKS INTO COMEBACKS

D r. Paul Stoltz is one of the nation's most renowned researchers on adversity. In his book *Adversity Quotient: Turning Obstacles into Opportunities,* he describes how we can determine our adversity quotient. The test reveals how well we deal with life's tough challenges, setbacks, and difficulties. When measuring a group of real estate salespeople, Stoltz found that agents with a high AQ outsold agents with a low AQ by as much as 250 percent.

Stoltz says people generally fall into three main categories: the quitter, the camper, and the climber. The quitters give up trying to live a purposeful life. According to Stoltz, "They refuse the opportunity and abandon the climb." In the second category, between 60 and 80 percent of people, are the campers. The campers only go so far and then "weary from the climb terminate their ascent." They set up camp somewhere along the road to success and may never see what else lies ahead on their journey. The climber is in the third category. Climbers are dedicated to a lifelong ascent, says Stoltz. These are resilient, tenacious, persistent people who don't know the meaning of the word quit. Typically, 5 to 20 percent of the people you work with are climbers.

Research by Dr. Martin Seligman shows that what counts is not what happens to us, it's how we interpret or explain an adverse event. Dr. Seligman measured the responses to adversity of thousands of insurance agents. He found that the way salespeople explained their difficulties—by using either optimistic or pessimistic terms—dramatically affected their sales results. Optimistic salespeople outsold pessimists by 88 percent. Salespeople who used pessimistic explanatory styles were three times more likely to quit regardless of talent.

To a sales manager, managing adversity is as important as managing goals. A successful sales team must strive to achieve ambitious goals and learn how to overcome obstacles. Unless a sales team develops a methodology for knocking down barriers and turning stumbling blocks into stepping-stones, a more resilient team will take the lead in the marketplace.

> **SUCCESS PRINCIPLE**
> Adversity is a slippery slope. That's why stick-to-itiveness is a prerequisite for reaching the top.

The sales manager has to apply the right mixture of realism and optimism to help salespeople understand that though they've lost a sale, they haven't lost their capacity to sell. The blueprint for managing adversity must be embedded in the manager's attitude. He or she has to demonstrate that we all can make the choice to respond to adversity in a positive, creative, and constructive way.

The most successful salespeople on any team are extraordinary climbers who conquer more difficulties than their competitors. Studies of people who have fought life's toughest battles show that winners over adversity discover inner peace, uncommon wisdom, and unprecedented levels of success.

Some experts suggest that we can fake it until we make it. There is some practical wisdom to that. Many feats of mankind hinge on a hope and a prayer. Sales success can hinge on the art of turning setbacks into comebacks. We alone hold the key to turning adversity into an excuse to camp out and fail or into a reason to continue the climb and win.

40

HOW TO MANAGE DISAPPOINTMENT

How do you handle disappointments? In business, the norm is to be upbeat, motivated, and achievement oriented. With everyone focused on success, disappointment can invite denial. According to Dr. Zaleznik, professor emeritus at the Harvard Business School, the way we handle disappointment is often more important in reaching success than our focus on success itself. Why? Because managing disappointment forces people to learn more about themselves and to better manage future disappointments. Here are some keys that can help you manage disappointment:

1. **Stop running.** Allow yourself time to think and sift through the residue of your troubling experience. If

you are alone, put it on paper. If you have a good friend, talk it over.

2. **Separate your ego from your loss.** If you lose a sale, you haven't lost your ability to sell. If you lose money, you haven't lost your capacity to work. No loss can turn you into a loser without your consent.

3. **Don't try to restore shattered dreams; build new dreams instead.** Accept the fact that we cannot revive, rebuild, or restore the past; we can only create a better future. New dreams create new hope.

4. **Align your dreams with your talents.** Dreams sometimes create the illusion that we have the talents to turn them into reality. Before you decide on a big dream, perform a "reality check." Ask successful people for help to appraise your talents objectively.

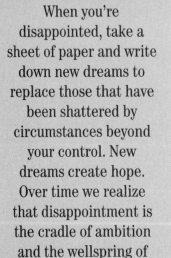

ACTION TIP

When you're disappointed, take a sheet of paper and write down new dreams to replace those that have been shattered by circumstances beyond your control. New dreams create hope. Over time we realize that disappointment is the cradle of ambition and the wellspring of bigger dreams.

5. **Develop a deeper commitment to meaningful goals.** If your commitment is only in your mind, then you'll lose it when you encounter a big obstacle. If your commitment is in your heart and your mind, you'll create the power to break through the toughest obstacles.

6. **Do not put all your eggs in one basket.** Successful salespeople always keep

their sales funnel filled with fresh opportunities. If one or two deals go sour, they have more in the wings.

7. **Create a balance in your life.** Lower your risks for suffering from disappointment. Create a balance among work, family, and play.

8. **Assign realistic probabilities to your expectations.** If you expect to win a large account, assign a percentage from 0 to 100 that reflects your chance of winning. If you believe that you have a 100 percent chance of winning with every account, your chances of suffering from disappointment will skyrocket.

9. **Learn and grow from every disappointment.** Don't sidestep growth by becoming cynical. Cynicism is the scar tissue of unresolved disappointment. Cynicism drives out the ability to look at the world optimistically.

10. **Learn from other people who have suffered from disappointment.** Disappointment managed well will often lead to greater success.

41

CHECK OUT YOUR
NEW EMPLOYER

Recently, one of my neighbors lost his job. The high-tech company he worked for as a regional sales manager was forced into bankruptcy. Although he knew that his employer was having financial difficulties, he blamed himself for not recognizing sooner that he had become a victim of poor management. Today he takes a much closer look at his prospective employers and says, "I don't want to make the same mistake twice."

What can sales executives do to avoid getting hurt by poor management practices? How can they evaluate the true opportunities a company can offer?

1. **Check the company's value system.** Read the company's mission statement. Ask about the company's philosophy of doing business, find out about the corporate culture and ethical guidelines, and ask how decisions are made that affect customers and salespeople (like price increases, customer complaints, or product improvements).

2. **Check management's commitment to progress.** Is the company committed to total quality? Does management pursue ongoing improvement? Are employees empowered to make decisions? How are employees trained to grow? What are the specific tools with which the company measures its progress?

3. **Check the company from the perspective of a customer.** Ask for the opportunity to visit a few of the company's customers. Ask a few questions about quality, service, follow-up, or ideas for improvement.

4. **Check the company from the perspective of an investor.** Since you are planning to invest your time, your energy, and your future, you should examine the company from the perspective of an investor who buys stock in the company. You are becoming a stakeholder in the company, and you want to make sure that if you create a certain value, you will receive a fair return on your investment.

5. **Check the company from the perspective of the owner.** Find out everything you can about the company's owner. Who started the company? Who owns the company now? Who runs the company today? What is the company's vision of the future? Find

out what influenced the company's growth (or decline) during the past five years.

6. **Check the company from the perspective of the reporter.** Go to the company's Website and click on "About Us." Read the company's history, read the press releases, learn about the key officers, and check their educational backgrounds. Next, search the Internet for articles

ACTION TIP

Check out the company's sales compensation system. Many new companies lure top salespeople from established firms with high salaries and unlimited earning potential. When these salespeople earn more than their managers, the company may change the commission system.

that have been published about the company. You'll find that many companies don't post all the articles written about them on their Websites. Search the Internet for articles that have been published about the company's officers. You'll be surprised how much you can learn about the company in a very short time.

The best companies to work for are those whose managers are well educated and that have a strong sense of loyalty to their customers, employees, and shareholders.

The more employees understand the role of management, the better they will be able to contribute and make their investment pay off.

42

SECRETS OF HIGH ACHIEVERS

I recently attended a seminar for company presidents. For a week I had the privilege of working closely with a group of high achievers who manage companies whose sales range from $10 million to $1 billion. Here are some of the characteristics of these high achievers.

1. **High achievers are driven by a pioneering spirit.** They explore uncharted territory, enjoy moving forward in the face of great risk, and love finding solutions to problems that others find daunting. They take pride in innovations that make old pathways to success obsolete.

2. **High achievers are impatient with those who**

seek safety and comfort. They prefer risk-taking to playing it safe. High achievers seek ever-greater challenges and aren't content with small, slow gains.

3. **High achievers know that all horizons are artificial.** When high achievers watch a sunset, they don't see the end of the day—they imagine the sun rising on the other side of the planet. They know that there is a new dawn every second somewhere on this earth.

4. **High achievers use a special compass to guide them.** Here are the four compass headings of the high achiever:

* **North.** High achievers climb higher. Austrian Reinhold Messner was the first human to set foot on 100 unexplored summits. He climbed Mount Everest solo, without oxygen, and mastered 14 of the tallest mountains in the world. Messner once described climbing as a theater of excellence.

* **South.** High achievers search deeper. When Alexander Graham Bell invented the telephone, cautious bankers dismissed the new device as "a curiosity that will not last." So he planned sales presentations where he would appear in one theater and talk to his assistant, Watson, in another. Bell knew that creating the telephone was not enough; he found new ways to sell his invention.

> **REMINDER**
>
> Here is the secret for staying ahead at all times: When reality forces you to take two steps back, think of new possibilities that will take you three steps forward.

172

- **West.** High achievers look far back. In *The Iliad,* the Greek poet Homer described tales of extraordinary heroes who lived 500 years earlier. When another high achiever, Heinrich Schliemann, read *The Iliad,* it motivated him to search for the lost city of Troy. Schliemann, who became wealthy as a military contractor during the Crimean War, devoted his later life to archeology and, in 1873, uncovered the treasures of Troy, once thought to be only a myth created by the Greek poet.

- **East.** High achievers look far ahead. Robert Zubrin of Pioneer Rocketplane recently described new airliners that will take off like jet planes and climb to 30,000 feet, where the pilot will ignite a rocket engine. Passengers will experience a 3-G acceleration and travel at a top speed of 13,000 mph. Flying time between New York and Tokyo will be 90 minutes. Who will be flying in the first rocket plane? I suspect it will be high achievers, daring pioneers who only think about possibilities—never limitations.

By using the high achiever's compass, you can shift the paradigm of your destiny.

43

IS LIFE AN ADVENTURE FOR YOU?

Research suggests that what CEOs do in their spare time influences their company's ability to grow. I've met many CEOs who flaunt their passion for thrills and live to tell about it. Why do some people swim with sharks, go skydiving, or try to set a world record in a hot-air balloon? Here are some possible explanations.

1. **It's an image booster.** Let's face it, a breathtaking tale about sailing in a typhoon, as Oracle founder Larry Ellison did, is going to get more attention in the boardroom than a story about a volleyball tournament.

2. **Some brains crave arousal.** Dr. Randy Larsen at the University of Michigan says that high-sensation seekers not only tolerate high stimulus well, but also crave it. To them, a plunge from a bridge is a plunge into adrenaline pleasure.

3. **It's our nature.** Dr. Frank Farley believes that we are a nation of thrill seekers. The United States is largely inhabited by descendants of immigrants who uprooted themselves to come to the New World.

4. **Thrill seekers go to the edge to find new solutions.** For example, Joe Liemandt, CEO of Trilogy, took a group of new employees to Las Vegas and urged them to bet a few thousand dollars of their company's money on a single spin of the roulette wheel. Although the group lost money, every employee learned that at Trilogy you don't get punished if you take a risk and lose.

5. **Thrill seekers declare war on fear.** One executive who likes climbing frozen waterfalls said that it helped him conquer his fear of death, saying, "I open the door, see the Grim Reaper right there, but instead of just slamming the door, you push him back a few steps."

6. **It's about being "in the zone."** Psychologist Beverly Potter suggests that thrill seekers pursue the unique sensation that comes only with optimal performance—when there is the right balance between difficulty and ability. Thrill seekers want to be right on the edge of control without losing it. When they reach that point, they are in the moment and experience "flow."

No matter what the reason for pursuing thrills, it appears that CEO's who seek thrills are good for business.

Ian MacMillan, a professor at Wharton, believes that many successful business leaders begin their thrilling journey to success with what he calls "entrepreneurial insight." While thrill seekers get an adrenaline rush from courting physi-

REMINDER

We all live with an invisible countdown clock. With every second that passes, we have one second less to live than a second earlier. Decide to make your life a memorable adventure.

cal danger, success seekers in business can experience the same excitement while launching a new business. Eager to turn their idea into reality, entrepreneurs are willing to embrace uncertainty and laugh at the possibility of loss. Fred Smith, the founder of Federal Express, felt the thrill of success when his first plane took off with a dozen packages from Memphis. Michael Dell, the founder of Dell Computers, experienced the high of assembling his first computer in a college dorm.

When a business idea takes root in the mind of an entrepreneur, it is hard to tell if the person owns the idea or the idea owns the person. Richard Branson, CEO of Virgin Atlantic Airlines, once said, "Being an adventurer and an entrepreneur are similar. You're willing to go where most people won't dare." Branson, who risked his life trying to circle the globe in a hot-air balloon, believes that risk taking is not about thrill seeking, "it's about not wasting one's life."

44

HOW TO CREATE
WINNING ATTITUDES

D aniel Boorstin once wrote, "The great obstacle to discovering the shape of the earth, the continents and the ocean was not ignorance, but the illusion of knowledge." Many people think they fully understand the power of attitudes, but their results often suggest the opposite. Their illusion of knowledge stands in the way of progress. Here are five winning attitudes that have proven successful in business over time.

1. **Attitude toward selling.** Dr. Norman Vincent Peale once suggested that the salesperson's attitude toward self determines success or failure. "A negative attitude creates tiredness, which takes energy and

vitality out of you. Positive thoughts and images create a positive emotion. You can say, 'This is a great day. I am fortunate to sell a wonderful product. I look forward to meeting many interesting people today; I will be able to help some of these people and they will become my friends. I look forward to learning a great deal today.' Thinking and talking that way adds to your enthusiasm and vitality."

2. **Attitude toward managing.** Cofounder of Amway Rich DeVos describes the winning attitude for sales managers to adopt: "The sales manager is caught somewhere between being a boss and being an inspirational leader. He or she has to show by example what it is possible to do. A sales manager has to be a trainer, a manager, a counselor and a hand holder and then has to help his or her people to be all they can be."

3. **Attitude toward the team.** Basketball coach Pat Riley feels that the key attitude is wanting to help other people. "Everybody has the natural desire to take care of 'me.' People are primarily selfish individuals. They don't really care about the team. They will voice a lot of insincere attitudes about wanting to help the team, but they really want to help themselves. If you can, find people who really want to be a part of a great team, of something significant, to do something for others, for their teammates and have an attitude and a passion that

SUCCESS PRINCIPLE

Attitudes drive skills, and the persistent application of attitudes and skills creates outstanding results.

doesn't depend on money. These people know that if they continue to chase the dream and really believe in what they're doing, the money and rewards will follow them."

4. **Attitude toward the company.** Stephen Covey once said that the common attitude of corporations is to create rules and regulations at the price of freedom and initiative. "So what's the solution? To come up with a set of principles and a common vision that everybody can buy into—and then to make people accountable. When you get enough people with information, you raise the consciousness and unleash energies. For the principle-centered leader, information then becomes power: the power of a collective will to accomplish the mission of the organization."

5. **Attitude toward the customer.** Many organizations tend to listen to their customers before the sale and then ignore them after the sale. Author Richard C. Whiteley suggests in his book, *The Customer Driven Company, Moving from Thought to Action,* "Saturate your company with the voice of the customer. Create real intimacy between yourself and the customers."

45

WHO CREATES HAPPINESS
FOR YOU?

One of the key goals of any salesperson is to create more happy customers. The logic is compelling. Since happy customers will give us more of their business, they will refer us to more of their friends and, as a result, we will do better. Plato once wrote, "He who does well must of necessity be happy." That thought brings up two questions: "Are you doing well?" and "Are you happy?" If the answer is "Yes" to both questions, skip this article. If you think you are doing well, but feel a lack of happiness, then we have two problems to discuss. One: How can you continue to make other people happy if you are unhappy? Two: What can you do to be happier?

Before we go any further, let's define what we mean by happiness. One of the difficulties in defining happiness lies in our forever-shifting awareness. For example, when we are completely healthy, we are not aware of our bodies. The same is true with happiness. When we are completely happy, we don't lack anything and we ignore our capacity to be unhappy. It is only when we are unhappy that we are aware of both—our unhappiness and our longing to be happy. Many people associate happiness with pleasure. Although pleasure can lighten unhappy moments, happiness is the result of long-term meaning. Whenever we engage in work that we really love to do, we will always lose track of time and feel an abundance of energy.

What can we do to become happier? Instead of finding happiness for themselves, some people spend more time making others believe that they are happy. They delude themselves by assuming that we always become what we think about. They forget that happiness is not an act of will, but an action skill. When we're engaged in a meaningful task where we exercise our basic skills, we lose our sense of time and forget about our capacity to be unhappy.

Many unhappy people think that getting away from their troubles holds the key to their happiness. The daily pressures of holding a job; the inconsiderate demands of family members; and the uncertainty of raising children in a society riddled by drugs, crime, and unemployment often wear down the most cheerful person. While trouble often spoils happiness, the French writer Montaigne suggested the bold idea that inner happiness can exist no matter how severe the troubles on the outside. Montaigne wrote in

1570, "When the city of Nola was ruined by the Barbarians, Paulinus, who was bishop of that place, having there lost all he had, and himself a prisoner, prayed after this manner: 'Oh Lord, defend me from being sensible of this loss; for Thou knowest they have yet touched nothing of that which is mine.' "

> **SUCCESS PRINCIPLE**
>
> Self-leadership doesn't require superhuman strength; it requires only discipline and commitment. The only one strong enough to hold you back from being happy and successful is you.

I remember conducting interviews with American pilots who were shot down over North Vietnam. Although they spent many years in prison camps, were tortured, malnourished, and deprived of the most elementary conveniences of modern life, they all felt sorry—not for themselves—but for their captors. Why? Because they knew that none of the prison guards had ever experienced freedom. Through it all, these POWs maintained their capacity to be happy.

Montaigne suggested that we all should reserve a sacred space in our hearts or minds, "a backshop wholly our own and entirely free, wherein to settle our true liberty." It is in this sacred inner space where we store our greatest treasures and hide them from decay or violence.

46

GOLF AS A CLOSING TOOL

About five years ago, I took up golf. I'm glad I did. The game opened a new world and also had a beneficial effect on business. In the beginning I went to the driving range as often as I could and immediately liked hitting the ball as hard as I could. Although I was a little worried about my first actual round of golf, a friend had the courage to take me out on a course in Scottsdale, Arizona, and I remember hitting more cactus plants than fairways. I'll never forget the score: 72 on the front nine and exactly the same on the back nine. I gave myself credit for consistency.

Soon I found that the word *golf* can be a great icebreaker and concluded that it pays to play. Golf not only brings out the child in the customer, it also makes pretense

ACTION TIP

Write your clients' hobbies in your contact management or CRM program. When you see an interesting article that relates to someone's hobby, send it to that client with a brief note.

and masks disappear. When customers hit a bad drive and the ball disappears in the woods, do they lose their temper? Do they cheat? You can judge people's characters very quickly when you observe how they handle pressure on the golf course.

A year ago, I played a round of golf with a CEO who approached us to do business with his company. During four and one-half hours of playing golf, I learned that this person was honest, highly competitive, personally encouraging, and generous in spirit. After a year of working with his company, the initial character reading turned out to be very accurate.

Over time, I've found that a $120 round of golf with a job applicant gives a more accurate reading than a $120 psychological test report. However, while you can get a good "read" on your customers by playing golf with them, make no mistake: Your customers will also watch you like a hawk. When they ask, "What was your score?" chances are they're testing your honesty.

It took me a while to realize that little things mean a lot on the golf course. I'm still embarrassed when I think of the time a friend explained to me that I had just walked over a customer's line of putt. I had no idea that my footprints could make an impression on the green and cause a ball to miss the hole.

Figuring out people appears to be a lot easier than understanding the idiosyncrasies of your own game. But what counts most, in business as in golf, is the bottom line. It took me no time at all to realize that golf is a great closing tool. I remember when I traveled with one of our salespeople to visit a "tough" account. When we sat down, I noticed a putter in the corner of the room. I used the magic word *golf*, and within seconds the prospect set up a target in the form of a coffee mug, and we happily practiced putting in his office. The game of golf created an instant bond; we closed a $22,000 sale; and I understood what the saying "Drive for show and putt for dough" means.

47

PUTTING LESSONS

I recently played in a charity golf tournament. One of the players hit a powerful drive on the 18th hole that split the fairway; he followed with a long, straight iron shot that rolled onto the green. Flushed with anticipation of a birdie, he lined up the six-foot putt and missed the hole by two feet. He had casually walked up and struck the ball without stopping. It rolled straight at first, then took a slight turn and rolled right past the hole. His face turned red. He hoped for a birdie, screwed up an easy par, and ended up with a bogey. Many golfers have experienced that agonizing moment. Many important matches have been lost this way. That's why golfers say, "If you can't putt, you can't win."

The same is true in selling. How we approach the cus-

> **SUCCESS PRINCIPLE**
>
> A successful life depends on the ability to do meaningful work, on the ability to love unconditionally, and on the ability to lose yourself in play.

tomer is critical; how we read the business opportunity is vital; how we shape our strategy is important; but if we can't deploy the finesse to close the deal, all the brilliant efforts that preceded the close are futile.

The big money winners in golf follow some fundamental rules for putting. Surprisingly enough, these rules apply also to closing sales.

1. **Never use a putter until the ball is on the green.** Amateurs sometimes try, when some yards off the green, to roll their ball onto the green with the putter. The strategy hardly ever works. Salespeople who apply a closing technique before the customer is ready will rarely get the chance to conclude the sale.
2. **Study the roll of every green.** Salespeople need to carefully survey the emotional landscape of the prospect. It's better to read the prospect's intentions, motivations, and emotions than to analyze and dissect the logical content of the customer's statements.
3. **Never use force.** Pros putt with an easy, effortless, pendulum-like swing. Like the golf pro, a professional salesperson does not force a close on a customer.
4. **Keep your eyes directly over the ball.** When your head is not directly above the ball, it is much harder to line up the putter. Golf pros visualize the

path the ball will take from the putter to the hole before they strike the ball. Likewise, top salespeople always keep their eyes squarely focused on the customer's position in relation to the close.

5. **Don't rush.** If the putt has too much speed, the ball will bounce right over the hole. A fast-talking salesperson has little chance of turning an open-minded prospect into a customer. Top sales performers are able to select the right pace that is comfortable for everyone.

Many salespeople get too anxious when it comes to closing sales. Top sales professionals follow a process, and unlike my golfing partner, they don't allow their emotions to override that process. They confidently focus on the process that results in their progress.

48

IMPROVE YOUR GAME PLAN

What will be important to win? It's a challenging course with tight fairways and deep bunkers guarding the greens. Let's check out the basics before we take that first mulligan.

1. **Keep your eye on the ball.** One of the reasons why golfers don't hit the sweet spot is that they let their eyes wander. Sales executives must never lose their focus on their customers. Everyone on the team needs to be reminded that it is the customer who writes our checks, not the sales team.

2. **Focus on your strategy and avoid traps.** Remember, there are two games in golf: One game is in

the air; the other on the ground. Similarly, there are two games in selling: One is creating opportunities; the other is solving problems. Good sales managers are those who drive their team to find opportunities and help keep them out of trouble.

3. **Use power wisely.** My biggest problem with golfing is overkill. The harder I hit the ball, the shorter it flies. My goal is to use less force and more finesse. Many sales managers tend to use too much force and too little finesse. Next time you need to make adjustments in your team, address the issue squarely, but use a gentle grip.

4. **Practice if you want to do better.** The best way to lower your score by five strokes is to practice for a half-hour before every game. Likewise, good sales managers periodically spend a half-hour with each salesperson on the team to improve their scores. We can only grow sales continuously if we are committed to continuous learning.

5. **Keep pace with the team ahead of you.** Imagine a round of golf where every foursome on the course spends five minutes searching for errant balls on every hole. The moment a sales team slows down, the entire company begins to suffer. Your customers expect a high speed of execution, while your competitors can't wait to catch up. Many

> **REMINDER**
>
> There should be no rules when it comes to envisioning a greater future, but to live successfully in the present, we need to play by the rules.

times the competition will get that $5,000 sale while your team is busy searching for a $2 ball.

6. **Repair your ball marks.** Everyone enjoys putting on a smooth surface, but not everyone likes to bend over and fix the marks the balls leave on the green. Remember that your team is entitled to play on a well-groomed course. Good managers know how to smooth ruffled feathers and repair bruised egos. Keep a level playing field and maintain the highest standards of integrity to prevent damage to the reputation of your company.

7. **Help your stars perform at their best.** Sometimes sales managers try to compete with their top sales stars instead of helping them win. This is not productive. For example, if I were forced into a one-hole playoff with Tiger Woods, I would tell him that I could predict the outcome and would offer to carry his clubs and watch him play.

$$\boxed{49}$$

AVOID GETTING SQUEEZED

With the economy still sputtering and CEOs keeping a tight lid on spending, sales managers report that paths to decision makers are blocked with obstacles. This is frustrating for the entire sales team, so I spoke with a number of seasoned managers to get a firsthand report, along with coping strategies. Below are the top six lessons gleaned from these managers.

1. **Real opportunities are harder to identify.** Most sales managers direct their salespeople to explore opportunities with companies that are doing well. What happens many times is that salespeople are not doing so well in capturing these opportunities.

ACTION TIP

When sales slow down, think of three things that are in your control that you can speed up. You can call more new prospects; you can call more existing clients; and you can ask for more referrals or think of new selling ideas. There is no slowdown for people who can think on their feet.

Why? Because the decision-making process has migrated upward, and salespeople are struggling to make connections with these upper-level executives. What's the solution? Bring higher-level executives to make joint calls with your salesperson.

2. Real solutions are harder to justify. Many times salespeople propose a great solution that will do wonders for their client. The only problem is that the client does not see enough benefits to justify the purchase. Why? Because many companies, still in a budget-saving mode, don't even think beyond the current quarter. The solution: Spend more time mapping the pain points in the earlier phases of the call. Ask the client to put a dollar figure next to each pain. Justify the economic wisdom of your solution by using your client's numbers.

3. **Friendly relationships are not always productive.** Some salespeople work hard on making every call a pleasant experience. Yet they are often surprised when a competitor calls on their client and walks away with a sale, leaving them empty handed. Why? Because some salespeople have a strong need to be liked, and their need for approval prevents them from asking some of the tough questions that would

advance the sale and actually help the customer make a favorable decision. The solution: Get these salespeople to switch from the "farming" style to the "hunting" style. If coaching fails, move them to customer service.

4. **With sales being slow, it's more difficult to cut off problem clients.** While sales managers preach that every sale counts, they often fail to count the time and expense it takes to close certain sales. The solution: Give your sales team clear directions for when to say no to a client.

5. **When business is slow, creative ideas are harder to find.** While it's easy to say that sales problems are nothing but wake-up calls for creativity, salespeople are often hard-pressed to come up with new ideas for increasing sales. Why? Because they think that they've tried everything under the sun. The solution: Pull in your top performers and list all the best ideas that worked for them. Then ask your top performers to act as mentors to your sales team.

6. **When business shrinks, salespeople get confused about your expectations.** Why? In tough times salespeople worry more about their jobs and their income. The solution: Don't add to their stress with unrealistic expectations or ambiguous leadership. Offer a clear vision of the future and create a solid plan that leads to new opportunities. Salespeople respect what you fairly expect and impartially inspect.

50

HOW EFFECTIVE ARE YOUR
SALES CALLS?

The best people in any profession work efficiently and effectively. The best carpenters make the fewest chips. Time and motion studies of world-class soccer players reveal that the top-rated players run far shorter distances and score more goals during a game than their less successful colleagues. At his peak level, basketball star Michael Jordan always gave 100 percent of himself in every game, yet he always had a little power reserve that he accumulated by playing efficiently. While poor performers turn part of their energy into waste, top performers save up energy and invest it effectively in last-minute, victory-saving bursts of performance.

Management experts will tell you that it is better to be effective than efficient. According to Daniel Stamp, the founder of Priority Management Systems, effectiveness is doing the right thing, whereas efficiency is doing things right. To improve our sales results, we need to improve both efficiency and effectiveness.

Here are three simple principles to remember when you meet your next customer:

1. **First, an effective listener sells more than an efficient talker.** The better you listen to your prospect, the less time it will take you to pinpoint the essence of your prospect's needs. Remember the soccer player who runs less but scores more goals? As you listen more effectively, you won't chase the sale; you'll allow the sale to come to you. As an effective listener you won't answer questions that were never asked or present solutions that don't fit the customer's problem.

2. **Second, your customers' erroneous beliefs weigh more in their minds than a prize bull at the state fair.** Psychologist Robert Abelson once proposed the idea that we treat beliefs like material possessions. Customers form their beliefs with great care, and they don't want you to shatter them. What do top performers do when they face erroneous beliefs such as "The competitor's product is

> **REMINDER**
>
> If you don't ask questions that lead you to the customer's needs, you won't be needed by your customer or your company.

better"? They don't challenge their customer's beliefs. A more effective strategy is to shift the focus back from the solution to the original problem. Instead of proving to the customer that they don't have the right solution, they lead their customers to carefully review the true nature of their problem. When customers review and restate their problem, it will often change in their minds. Once the problem definition changes, chances are that the competitive solution will no longer fit and the effective salesperson can introduce a far better solution.

3. **Third, it is more effective to pull the toughest problems out of a prospect's mind than to push the best solution.** The toughest job in selling is to find, isolate, and clearly define your prospect's real problem. Chances are that your prospect has not had the time to clearly define the problem at hand. Top performers know that an inefficient analysis of a problem will lead to an inefficient solution. If you spend more time agreeing with the customer on the problem, you will spend less time selling the solution. Why? Because a clearly stated problem takes away the customer's confusion—and as a result, the customer will think of you as the more effective salesperson and buy from you. Isn't it more efficient to be effective?

51

CADILLAC DREAMS

In Europe where I grew up, we always associated the name Cadillac with the best of the best. In my home country, Austria, American automobiles were a novelty. A privileged few owned Ford Mustangs. You could see American tourists in Buicks and Chevrolets, but only the wealthiest Austrians cruised the streets of Salzburg in a Cadillac. Mr. Winkler, the owner of the city's largest hotels, became the best-known car owner in town by treating himself to a brand-new Cadillac every year. His latest model always made newspaper headlines in Salzburg.

I was still riding a bicycle when I first studied Mr. Winkler's car up close, wondering just how many horses were harnessed by this sleek metal sculpture on wheels. For me, a Cadillac was the stuff of dreams. Over the years, I learned more about Cadillac's amazing achievements. The company's steady pursuit of quality and continuous search for ongoing improvement earned Cadillac an enviable place in automotive history. For example, Cadillac was the first car company to replace the unwieldy hand-crank starter with an electric starter for its 1912 models.

This idea originated at National Cash Register, the company that spawned modern selling techniques. NCR engineer Charles Kettering developed an electric motor that provided short bursts of power for cash registers. When Cadillac hired him, Kettering adapted his idea to car engines. His battery-powered starter kept Cadillac sales soaring.

When I moved to America, I first bought a Volkswagen, a decision I soon regretted, since it had no air conditioning. Two years later, I switched to an American coupe and then to a station wagon to accommodate the demands of a growing family. As our business expanded and prospered, my nostalgia for Cadillac cars drove me to trade in my station wagon for a sleeker and more businesslike Seville.

The Cadillac salesman, a 25-year veteran of car sales, convinced me that I deserved to turn my Austrian/American dream into reality. He pointed out that I deserved the very highest standard of quality.

To me the name Cadillac represents more than quality, the Baldrige Award, or Gold Key service. The Cadillac crest is a symbol of the pioneering and leadership qualities of its namesake, Antoine de la Mothe Cadillac, who was born in France in 1658 and came to America to found a settlement he called La Ville d'Etroit in 1701, which later became the Motor City, Detroit.

When I took a test drive in the new Seville to get a feel of the famous Northstar engine, it was a thrill. I slipped in a CD, took a whiff of the new car smell, and for a brief moment I felt like Mr. Winkler and realized that quality cars are not only a means of transportation, but a means of transformation.

> **SUCCESS PRINCIPLE**
>
> If somebody with a name that nobody can pronounce can come to this country with no money and start a magazine and actually succeed, what does that tell you? Those who feel they have nothing to lose are the least afraid of taking a risk.

While many people like to sing while they are driving, I like to think of famous movie lines. As I drove down the highway the first line that came to my mind was that of a comedian named Smirnoff: "America, what a country!" A country built by immigrants who dared to dream.

INDEX

© Hisham Bharoocha

About the Author

A dual citizen of both Austria and the United States, Gerhard Gschwandtner is the founder and publisher of *Selling Power,* the leading magazine for sales professionals worldwide, with a circulation of 165,000 subscribers in 67 countries.

He began his career in his native Austria in the sales training and marketing departments of a large construction equipment company. In 1972, he moved to the United States to become the company's North American Sales Training Director, later moving into the position of Marketing Manager.

In 1977, he became an independent sales training consultant, and in 1979 created an audiovisual sales training course called "The Languages of Selling." Marketed to sales managers at Fortune 500 companies, the course taught nonverbal communication in sales together with professional selling skills.

In 1981, Gerhard launched *Personal Selling Power,* a tabloid format newsletter directed to sales managers. Over the years the tabloid grew in subscriptions, size, and frequency. The name changed to *Selling Power,* and in magazine format it became the leader in the professional sales field. Every year *Selling Power* publishes the "Selling Power 500," a listing of the 500 largest sales forces in America. The company publishes books, sales training posters, and audio and video products for the professional sales market.

Gerhard has become America's leading expert on selling and sales management. He conducts webinars for such companies as SAP, and *Selling Power* has recently launched a new conference division that sponsors and conducts by-invitation-only leadership conferences directed toward companies with high sales volume and large sales forces.

For more information on *Selling Power* and its products and services, please visit www.sellingpower.com.

Subscribe to *Selling Power* today and close more sales tomorrow!

GET 10 ISSUES – INCLUDING *THE SALES MANAGER'S SOURCE BOOK*.

In every issue of *Selling Power* magazine you'll find:

■ **A Sales Manager's Training Guide** with a one-hour sales training workshop complete with exercises and step-by-step instructions. Get a new guide in every issue! Created by proven industry experts who get $10,000 or more for a keynote speech or a training session.

■ **Best-practices reports** that show you how to win in today's tough market. Valuable tips and techniques for opening more doors and closing more sales.

■ **How-to stories** that help you speed up your sales cycle with innovative technology solutions, so you'll stay on the leading edge and avoid the "bleeding edge."

■ **Tested motivation ideas** so you and your team can remain focused, stay enthusiastic and prevail in the face of adversity.

NEW! Digital Edition same as print. 100% online.

Plus, you can sign up for five online SellingPower.com newsletters absolutely FREE.

FOR FASTEST SERVICE CALL 800-752-7355
TO SUBSCRIBE ONLINE GO TO WWW.SELLINGPOWER.COM

I want a one-year subscription to *Selling Power* magazine.

☐ **YES!** Send me one year of the print edition for only $27
☐ **YES!** Sign me up for one year of the digital edition for only $19
☐ **YES!** Sign me up for one year of both for only $33

Please note: Subscriptions begin upon receipt of payment. For priority service include check or credit card information. Canadian and overseas subscriptions, please visit www.sellingpower.com for rates.

Name: _____ Title: _____

Company: _____

Address:_____

City: _____ State: _____ Zip: _____ Phone: _____

☐ Check enclosed   Charge my ☐ Visa ☐ MC ☐ AMEX ☐ Discover

Card number: _____ Exp.:_____

Name on card: _____ Signature: _____

For fastest service call 800-752-7355 • To subscribe online go to www.sellingpower.com